For my Mom
who taught me how to knit
more than just scarves.

BEYOND THE SCARF

15 Simple & Fun Fashions You Can Knit

Kathleen Greco & Nick Greco

Published by C&T Publishing, Inc., P.O. Box 1456, Lafayette, CA, 94549; and Dimensional Illustrators, Inc., 362 Second Street Pike #112, Southampton, PA, 18966, Phone: (215) 953-1415 Email: yummyyarns@3dimillus.com,

Website: www.jellyyarn.com

Front cover: Chenille Ruffle Top
Back cover: Spring Sweater, Cozy Capelet, Easy Skirt

Library of Congress Cataloging-in-Publication Data

Greco, Kathleen.

Beyond the scarf : 15 simple & fun fashions you can knit / Kathleen Greco & Nick Greco.

p. cm.

Includes index.

ISBN-13: 978-1-57120-383-0 (paper trade : alk. paper)

ISBN-10: 1-57120-383-4 (paper trade : alk. paper)

1. Knitting--Patterns. 2. Scarves. I. Greco, Nick. II. Title.

TT825.G6825 2006

746.43'20432--dc22

2006010005

ISBN 10: 1-57120-383-4
ISBN 13: 978-1-57120-383-0

Printed in China 10 9 8 7 6 5 4 3 2 1

Publisher **Amy Marson**

Editorial Director **Gailen Runge**

Acquisitions Editor **Jan Grigsby**

Creative Director / Creative Editor **Kathleen Greco** *Dimensional Illustrators, Inc.*

Executive Editor **Nick Greco** *Dimensional Illustrators, Inc.*

Book Design and Typography **Deborah Davis** *Deborah Davis Design*

Knitwear Designs **Kathleen Greco** *Dimensional Illustrators, Inc.*

Fashion Photographer **Joe VanDeHatert** *Studio V*

Knitting and Yarn Photography **Kathleen Greco** *Dimensional Illustrators, Inc.*

Knitting Consultants **Karen Greenwald and Maria Williams**

Knitters **Lisa Gibson and Dr. Gail G. Cohen**

Acknowledgments
Special thanks to Amy Marson, Gailen Runge, and Jan Grigsby at C&T Publishing. A very special thank you to Deborah for her stunning designs. Our appreciation to Joe VanDeHatert for his outstanding fashion photography, and to all our models for their poise, style, and grace. Thanks Lisa and Gail for your knitting artistry. We are very grateful to Karen and Maria for their inspiration and advise. Thanks to the many yarn companies for their generosity. All our love to our dear family.

–Nick and Kathleen Greco

Table of Contents

Beyond the Scarf Projects
28

Introduction

There is an element of satisfaction when completing a knitted scarf. It's quick, easy, and always in fashion. We go beyond the level of scarf-making, with easy projects that incorporate new techniques, and provide new and beginner knitters a greater sense of accomplishment. You can knit the wardrobe that matches your flair for fashion.

In Chapter 1, all the basic knitting patterns are here from start to finish including making a slipknot, casting on, knit, and purl stitches, increasing, decreasing, binding off, as well as, finishing and assembly.

With Chapter 2, you'll learn about novelty yarns and find practical tips for knitting with the latest fashion fibers. We'll show you how to pair yarns, that when knitted, create wonderful textural fabrics that resemble complex stitch patterns.

In Chapter three, your skills will advance with each project, as you progress through the book. Three fashionable Easy projects get you started in simple Garter and Stockinette stitch patterns including an elegant self-fringing wrap, a slick belt, and fashion beaded Flip-flops. The next six Beginner projects guide you through easy shaping, and minimal finishing with two trouble-free sleeveless tops, a mini ruffle-edged poncho, two fashion purses, and an indispensable beach bag. In the last six Advanced Beginner projects, we'll increase your fashion wardrobe and skills with defined shaping, knitting with beads, and moderate assembly. Learn to knit a simple short-sleeved sweater, capelet and skirt ensemble, lacework top, beaded handbag, and a sassy little black shrug.

Beyond the Scarf provides fresh techniques for new knitters, expands beginner knitter's knowledge, enhances your knitting repertoire, and gives you the ability to go far beyond simple scarves. So, if you're ready for a fun experience, pick up your needles, select a favorite project, and let's get started!

Learn to Knit

This chapter teaches first-time knitters the basic knitting stitches, and provides a refresher for beginner knitters.

Color photographs guide you through the essentials of knitting beginning with a slipknot, casting on, knitting, purling, increasing, decreasing, and binding off. Progress to valuable fresh techniques, that demonstrate knitting with beads, and how-to attach handles easily, and efficiently.

Learn the importance that gauge, tension, and needle size play on the final dimensions of your finished garment, and how to read, and understand, a knitting pattern. End with finishing, and assembly methods, from weaving loose ends, to putting all the pieces together. Basic decorative stitch patterns including Garter, Stockinette, Ribbing, and Seed are discussed and displayed. With practice, you'll be ready to relax, have fun, and enjoy the art of knitting.

KNITTING BASICS

Gauge

Gauge is the number of stitches and rows over a standard dimension. If the number of stitches is greater than the pattern, your stitches are too small and you should use larger needles. If the number of stitches is fewer than the pattern, your stitches are too big and you should use smaller needles. Remember: Follow the suggested gauge to guarantee your garment will fit properly.

Tension

Tension refers to how tight or how loose your stitches are on the needle. Tension and gauge have a direct relationship to the size of the garment you are knitting. Always knit a 4" x 4" test swatch to ensure the gauge matches the knitting pattern.

Reading a Knitting Pattern

Patterns are written in shorthand using common knitting abbreviations, terms, and symbols. Practice will help you read knitting instructions easily. Patterns include: Skill level, needle sizes, yarn needed, sizes, gauge, stitch pattern and row-by-row instructions.

Skill Level—Beginner

Has mastered the techniques of knitting and purling.

Needles

Needles are available in size US #1 (2.25mm) to size US #50 (25.50mm)
For example: US #9 (5.5mm) needles

Yarn

For example: 2 balls Trendsetter Yarns *Perla*, 84yds (76m) 20g (100% Polyester) Color: #55

Sizes

A project with multiple sizes is written in brackets.

For example: Bust 34 (36, 38, 40)"

Gauge

For example: In Stockinette Stitch Pattern, 12 sts and 20 rows = 4"

*Asterisks

Asterisks mean for example: *K2, P4 repeat from * 4 times. After completing the instructions 1 time, repeat instructions between the asterisks 4 more times. A total of 5 times.

Brackets

[ ] Brackets are substituted for asterisks.
[K2, P2] 3 times means, K2 stitches, then P2 stitches a total of 3 times.

Parentheses

( ) Parentheses indicate size, number of stitches or inches.

For example: Size: 8 (10, 12, 14), Stitches: 26 (28, 30, 32), Inches: 4 (6, 8, 10)". Patterns are written in parentheses according to size from smallest to largest.

Can you read this pattern?

With US #10 needles and Fashion Trend yarn, CO 36 (38, 40, 42) sts. Work in Garter Stitch patt for 10 rows. Change to US #11 needles and *Poof* yarn. Working in St st, dec 10 sts evenly across 1st row = 26 (28, 30, 32) sts. Work even until piece measures 13 (14, 15, 16)" Next row: BO 6 (7, 7, 8) sts. Work 14 (14, 16, 16) sts. BO last 6 (7, 7, 8) sts. Reattach yarn at neck edge. Work 3 (5, 5, 5) rows. BO loosely.

ABBREVIATIONS

Below is a list of common abbreviations used in this text. Remember to read each pattern completely before you begin knitting.

bk lp – back loop
BO – bind off
CO – cast on
col – color
cont – continue
dec – decrease
Garter st – knit or purl every row
gm – gram
inc – increase
" or in – inch
K – knit
K1 tbl – knit one stitch through back loop
k2tog – knit 2 stitches together (right-slanting decrease)
kfb – knit into front and back of same stitch (to increase)
LH – left-hand
oz – ounce
P – purl
patt – pattern
pfb – purl into front and back of same stitch (to increase)
pm – place ring marker
psso – pass slipped stitch over
pwise – purlwise
p2tog – purl 2 stitches together (right-slanting decrease)
p2tog tbl – purl 2 stitches together through back loop
rep – repeat
rep from * – repeat instruction after *
RH – right-hand
rev St st – reverse stockinette stitch (purl 1 row, knit 1 row)
rnd – round
sl st – slip stitch
Sl 1 K – slip I stitch knitwise
Sl 1 P – slip 1 stitch purlwise
Sl 1, K1, PSSO or SKP – slip 1 stitch, knit 1 stitch, pass slipped stitch over. (left-slanting decrease)
st(s) – stitch(es)
St st – stockinette stitch (knit 1 row, purl 1 row; repeat)
tbl – through back loop

tog – together
work even – continue in pattern without increasing or decreasing
WS – wrong side
wyib – with yarn in back (knit stitch)
wyif – with yarn in front (purl stitch)
YO – yarn over

Needle Sizes

U.S.	Metric
0	2.00mm
1	2.25mm
2	2.75mm
3	3.25mm
4	3.50mm
5	3.75mm
6	4.00mm
7	4.50mm
8	5.00mm
9	5.50mm
10	6.00mm
10.5	6.50mm
11	8.00mm
13	9.00mm
15	10.00mm
17	12.75mm
18	14.00mm
19	15.00mm
35	19.00mm
50	25.50mm

SLIPKNOT

Begin knitting by making a basic slipknot. Tie the knot securely on the needle, but loose enough to allow the stitches to slide easily along the needle.

1. Make a slipknot by winding the yarn twice around your index and middle fingers.

2. To create a new loop, draw the yarn attached to the skein through the loop.

3. Insert the needle through the loop and tighten the knot on the needle. Make sure the slipknot is snug, but not tight. The slipknot is considered the first cast on stitch.

DOUBLE CAST ON

Casting on adds the number of stitches required to begin a pattern. The double cast on technique uses a tail, and the strand attached to the skein to cast on stitches on the needle.

1. Begin by wrapping the tail end around your left thumb clockwise and wrapping the skein yarn around your index finger counterclockwise to form a slingshot. Secure both strands securely in the palm of your left hand (LH).

2. Insert the needle under the strand on your thumb and lift yarn from the bottom with the tip of the needle.

3. Hook the needle behind the yarn on your index finger from top to bottom and draw the needle back through the loop on your thumb. Slip the loop off your thumb and gently tighten the stitch on the needle. Repeat steps 2 and 3 until the required number of stitches is cast on the needle.

KNIT STITCH

The knit stitch is one of two basic knitting stitches. When making a knit stitch, always keep the yarn in back of the needles. The letter K is the knitting symbol for the knit stitch. Master the knit stitch to make a basic Garter stitch fabric.

PURL STITCH

The purl stitch is the second basic knitting stitch. When making a purl stitch, keep the yarn in front of the needles. The letter P is the knitting symbol for the purl stitch. Learn the purl stitch to make the Stockinette stitch (Knit 1 row and Purl 1 row).

1. With the skein yarn in your right hand (RH) and the needle with the cast on stitches (slide stitches down to 1" from the tip) in your (LH), insert the RH needle from left to right, (knitwise). The RH and LH needles form an X.

1. With the yarn in front and the needle with the stitches in your LH, insert the (RH) needle through the first stitch from right to left, (Purlwise).

2. Always keep the yarn in back of the needles for a knit stitch. Wrap the yarn counterclockwise around the tip of the RH needle and gently pull the yarn down between the two needles.

2. The RH needle is above the LH needle and forms an X. Wrap the yarn counterclockwise around the tip of the RH needle.

3. Insert the tip of the RH needle up through the cast on stitch and lift the stitch off the LH needle. You have completed one knit stitch. Repeat all 3 steps until all the knit stitches are on the RH needle.

3. Carefully draw the tip of the RH needle back through the stitch and slide the original stitch off the LH needle. Repeat all 3 steps until all the purl stitches are on the RH needle.

DECREASING

Right-Slanting Decrease (/)

Knitting 2 stitches together produces stitches that slant to the right, and reduces the number of stitches by 1. The knitting symbol for this decreasing technique is K2tog.

Left-Slanting Decrease (\ )

Slip 1 stitch, knit 1 stitch, pass slipped stitch over produces stitches that slant to the left. The knitting symbol for this decrease technique is Sl 1, K1, PSSO or SKP.

1. Insert the RH needle from left to right (knitwise) into the next 2 stitches.

1. Insert the RH needle from left to right as if to knit and slip the stitch off the LH needle on to the RH needle.

2. Knit as usual keeping the yarn in back of the needles.

2. Knit the next stitch.

3. Lift the original 2 stitches off the LH needle. The stitches are reduced to 1 stitch on the RH needle. The result is a garment that slants to the right (/).

3. Lift the slipped stitch up over the knit stitch and completely off the RH needle. The result is a left-slanting decrease (\ ).

BAR INCREASE

Increasing stitches will make a garment wider. With this method, you knit into the front and back of the same stitch. The knitting symbols for increasing are inc or kfb (knit into front and back).

1. With the yarn in back, insert the RH needle knitwise and knit as usual. Do not slip the stitch off the LH needle.

2. Insert the RH needle into the back of the same stitch and knit as usual.

3. Slip the original stitch off the LH needle. You have made 2 stitches from 1 and completed a bar increase.

YARN OVER

The Yarn Over stitch is a technique that creates a decorative opening or eyelet in your knitted work. The yarn over demonstrated below is made between 2 knit stitches. The symbol for a yarn over is YO.

1. Bring the yarn forward between the needles.

2. Wrap the yarn around the right needle, from front to back, and return the yarn to the back.

3. Knit the next stitch. This creates a gap or hole between the 2 knit stitches and completes the yarn over.

BINDING OFF

Binding off prevents a knitted garment from unraveling. BO is the knitting symbol for binding off. This method secures the stitches on your knitwear and leaves a clean, decorative edge.

1. Knit or purl the first two stitches.

2. Insert the tip of the LH needle into the first stitch, lift the stitch over the second stitch and off the RH needle.

3. Knit or purl one stitch and repeat step 2 until one stitch remains on the LH needle. Lift the last stitch off the needle and cut the yarn, leaving a 6" tail. Thread the yarn through the last stitch and knot to complete the bind off. Weave in the tail.

KNITTING WITH BEADS

Beads add sparkle to any knitting project. It is very important that you choose beads that fit easily onto the yarn strand. When working with beads, remember to bring the yarn in front of a slip stitch on a right-side row. Beads add pop to tops, purses, and belts.

1. Bring ball yarn forward between the needles and slip the next stitch knitwise off the left-hand needle on to the right-hand needle.

2. Push the next bead in front of the slip stitch and pass the ball yarn to the back of the work, as if to knit.

3. Knit the next stitch. Repeat steps 1, 2, and 3 until all the beads are in position.

HANDLE WRAP TECHNIQUE

This is an efficient way to cast on, and bind off on a
U-shaped purse handle. The technique is specific to
the Boa Jelly Purse pattern on page 50, but can be
applied to other bulky fiber yarns, as well.

Handle Cast On	**Handle Bind Off**

1. Working 2 strands of Bulky Jelly Yarn® held together,
knot ends together, trim even, and begin cast on 54"
(137cm) from tail end of the yarn. Cast on 3 stitches
using long tail method. Before the 4th cast on stitch, pull
tail ends through 1st purse handle opening from back
to front, position yarn behind needle, and make taut.

2. Make a 4th cast on stitch. Pull tail ends through
handle opening, and cast on 2 stitches, make taut
each time = 6 total cast on stitches. Then, cast on 11
stitches = 17 total cast on stitches.

3. Before the 18th cast on, pull tail ends through
handle opening from back to front, position yarn
behind needle, cast on 18th stitch, and make taut.
Pull ends through handle opening, cast on 2 stitches,
make taut each time = 20 total cast on stitches. Then,
cast on 3 stitches = 23 total cast on stitches.

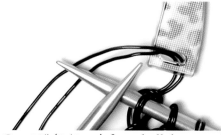

1. Cut 98" (249cm) from ball, knot ends, and trim
even. Knit 3, *Knit 1, pull ends through 2nd handle
opening from back to front, position yarn behind the
needle*, repeat from * to * 2 times, make taut each
time = 6 total stitches.

2. Knit across 11 stitches, to last 6 stitches = 17 total
stitches. *Knit 1, pull ends through handle opening
from the back to the front, then position the yarn
behind the needle* repeat from * to * 2 times, make
taut each time = 20 total stitches. Knit remaining 3
stitches = 23 total stitches.

3. Fold handle flat on outside of purse and BO
loosely.

GARTER STITCH PATTERN

The Garter stitch pattern is one of the most common patterns in knitting. Make it by either knitting every row, or purling every row. This pattern creates a fabric that has identical bumps on both sides. The Garter stitch is ideal for knitting scarves, purses, blankets, and simple tops.

Knit every row.

STOCKINETTE STITCH PATTERN

Knit a Stockinette stitch pattern by alternating between a row of knit and a row of purl stitches. This pattern creates V-shaped stitches on the right side, (the side worn on the outside) and bumpy stitches on the wrong side, (the side worn on the inside). Use it to knit tops, sweaters, shrugs, and wraps.

Row 1: K across.
Row 2: P across.
Repeat rows 1 and 2.

RIBBING STITCH PATTERN

A Ribbing stitch pattern produces an elastic edge that expands and returns to its original shape. Cast on an even number of stitches. Knit the stitches that were purled in the previous row, and purl the stitches that were knit in the previous row. It's ideal for making cuffs, neckbands, and waistbands.

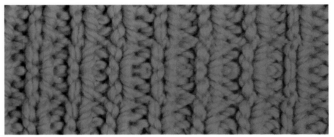

1 x 1 Ribbing (cast on multiples of 2) Row 1: *K1, P1. Repeat from * to end of row. Repeat this row

2 x 2 Ribbing (cast on multiples of 4) Row 1: *K2, P2. Repeat from * to end of row. Repeat this row

SEED STITCH PATTERN

Use the Seed stitch to make basic knit and purl decorative stitches. To create this pattern, cast on stitches in multiples of 2. In row 1, you alternate between knit and purl stitches. In row 2, reverse the process and alternate between purl and knit stitches.

Row 1: *K1, P1. Repeat from * to end of row.
Row 1: *P1, K1. Repeat from * to end of row.
Repeat rows 1 & 2.

MATTRESS STITCH

The Mattress Stitch is one of the easiest methods for joining knitted pieces. The result is a flexible, nearly invisible seam. This stitch requires that both pieces have an equal number of rows.

1. Line up the knitted garments side by side (right side facing) and thread a needle leaving a 6" tail. Insert the needle from back to front into the corner stitch two times to anchor the stitch.

2. Insert the needle under the horizontal bar between the two end stitches on the opposite side. Alternate sides below and above the horizontal bar.

3. Pull yarn ends to join, and weave in loose ends.

JOINING YARNS

Ultimately you will need more yarn, want to switch yarn, or change colors. To avoid bulging, join yarn at the end of a row. When you finish a project, weave the yarn ends into a seam.

Make a slipknot with the new yarn and pull the old yarn through the knot leaving a 6" tail. Holding the short tails in your LH, slide the slipknot up next to the needle and continue knitting.

WEAVING LOOSE ENDS

To achieve a professional look and prevent unraveling during washing, you will need to weave in all loose ends.

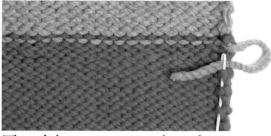

Thread the garment yarn through a tapestry or darning needle. Insert the needle through the loops along the edge of the knitted work and trim the yarn close to the surface.

All About Novelty Yarns

Discover the beauty, and uniqueness of novelty yarns. This chapter discusses the characteristics, and textural features of knitting with these enchanting yarns. We review the qualities of each of these fabulous trendsetting yarns, including Eyelash, Fur, Fuzz, Flat, Chunky & Funky, Multi-strand, Metallic and Jelly Yarns®. We answer the specific knitting questions, that will offer you a trouble-free experience. Common problems of knitting with novelty yarns are addressed including how-to see stitches clearly, keeping an accurate stitch count, and making a shoulder strap.

Explore the limitless textural possibilities of yarn pairing, and color coordinating. Full-color, sample fabrics are displayed, and various strand combinations are suggested. Color basics, for achieving great results when mixing yarns, are highlighted. Knitting with novelty yarns is both a fun, and challenging way of broadening your knitting experience, and enhancing the look, and quality of all the garments you choose to knit.

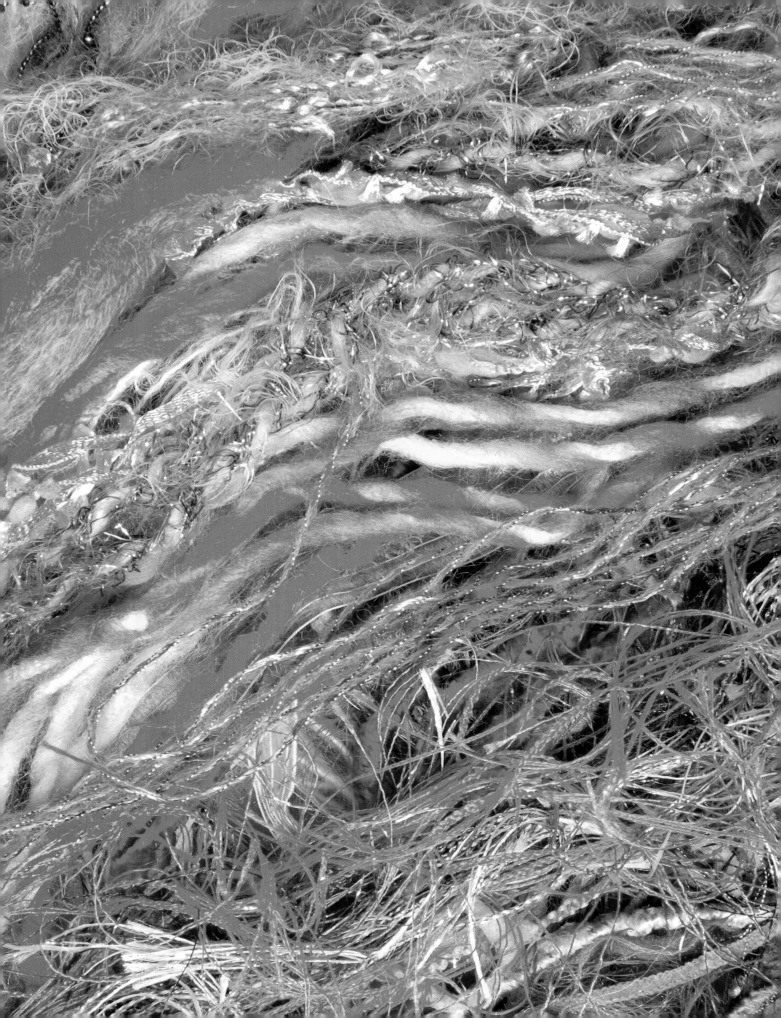

NOVELTY YARNS

Novelty yarns have become the newest fashion trend in knitting. Today, there are so many yarns to choose from, that they have become the most widely used, contemporary fibers. Each yarn has its own unique qualities, and characteristics, which when worked together, result in a plethora of unique textures.

We have classified these chic fashion yarns into eight distinct categories: Eyelash, Fur, Fuzz, Flat, Chunky and Funky, Multi-strand, Metallic, and Jelly Yarn®.

Eyelash

Eyelash is one of the most popular, super-fine weight yarns. It is composed of three, or more fibers evenly spaced along a base thread. Generally used as an accent yarn, these delicate strands add zest to any knitwear project.

Fur

This trendy yarn works well as an edging for trims or cuffs, and creates a luxurious, rich texture. After knitting each row or round with Fur yarns, gently comb the long fibers on the needle with a fine-toothed comb. Most furry yarns are very forgiving, and mistakes are rarely noticeable.

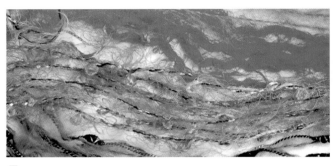

Fuzz

Fuzz yarns are a nappy, feathery-soft medium weight, which has the feel of mohair, or cashmere. While the texture resembles fine cashmere, it has the strength of wool and mohair.

Flat

Flat yarns are light to medium in weight, and are divided into three distinct categories: ladder, flag, and ribbon. Typical ladder yarns resemble railroad tracks, with two, thin parallel strands of thread, joined by crossbar fibers. Flag yarns consist of tufts of fiber strung along a strong core thread. Popular Ribbon yarns are wide and flat, look great when worked alone, and produce a spongy-soft texture.

NOVELTY YARNS

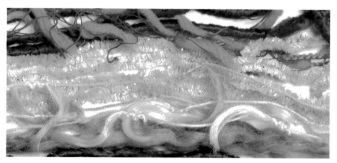

Chunky and Funky

These playful, eclectic yarns knit up well alone, or as a base with other novelty yarns. Surface texture and color are important elements when considering these yarns.

Multi-strand

Multi-strand yarns are a mixture of fibers, twisted onto one strand. These versatile fibers afford knitters an opportunity to use many yarns, without have to buy each yarn individually.

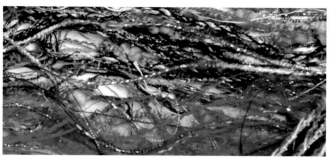

Metallic

Metallic yarns add sparkle and glitter to knitwear projects. These special yarns are embedded with metallic flecked fibers, intertwined with micro-metallic ply threads, or embedded with plastic reflective squares or circular sequins. Metallic yarns add glamour and glitter to every garment. These little gems are a great way of adding pop to a project.

Jelly Yarn®

Cool and modern Jelly Yarn® is the hottest yarn for contemporary knitters. The yarns are not cord or flat lanyard, but a round, pliable vinyl that is specially formulated for knitting and crochet. Available in Fine and Bulky weights, there are 7 different colors aptly named: Black Licorice, Blue Taffy, Pink Parfait, Raspberry Sorbet, Lemon-Lime Ice, Hot Pink Candy, and Orange Sherbet. The result is a glossy knitted fabric that is retro, with a techno flair.

In combination, these wonderful fashion yarns offer contemporary knitters the opportunity to experiment, with many different yarns, in an exciting, creative way.

KNITTING TRICKS AND TIPS

The patterns in *Beyond the Scarf* demonstrate new techniques, and methods for easy, trouble-free knitting. We all have different ways of streamlining our knitting. Below are a few of our favorite helpful tricks, and tips to facilitate your knitting experience, especially if you are a new knitter.

Do your bind off stitches appear curved rather than straight?

If you knit with a tight tension, your bind off stitches will appear curved and rigid. In some patterns, you may be able to bind off with a needle that's one size larger. By changing needles, your stitches will loosen, and your bind off row will be straighter.

How do you keep an accurate stitch count?

Ruffles require a large number of cast on stitches. After casting on, place stitch markers every 10 sts, align the stitches on the needle before beginning the first row or round, especially on circular needles. Remove markers after 1st row.

Do you have trouble seeing stitches on the needle?

With fur or fuzzy yarns it may be difficult to see individual stitches. Use contrasting color needles, and place stitch markers in between each cast on stitch. Slip the marker off onto the right-hand needle after each stitch. This may seem a bit slow, but it will help you keep an accurate stitch count, and prevents split stitches.

What is the best method for attaching handles?

Use the Handle Wrap technique (page 19) to knit U-shaped purse handles to your knitting with Jelly Yarn®. You can also apply this singular technique with with fiber yarns.

How much yarn is needed for the Long Tail cast on?

Do you hate running out of yarn when you're casting on? For several projects requiring a large amount of stitches, we have indicated where to begin the cast on, including: Easy Skirt, Cozy Capelet, Chenille Purse, Boa Jelly Bag, and Beaded Flip-flops. The rule is, allow 1" (2.5cm) of yarn for every cast on stitch. This will work for US #11 (8mm) through US #19 (15mm) needles; for US #35 (19mm) allow more; for needles under US #11 (8mm), allow a little less.

How to work shoulder straps…individually or together?

Should you work both straps at the same time or separately? The patterns in this book suggest that you work the shoulders separately. If you want to knit them at the same time follow this procedure: When you reach the last stitch on the first strap, tie the stitch with a strand from a new ball of yarn. When you turn and return, work the strap attached to the main ball of yarn, then work the other strap with the new ball of yarn. You will work both sides faster and evenly.

EXPLORING COLORS AND TEXTURES

Beyond the Scarf introduces you to an array of fashionable projects, knit with matching yarns in basic Garter, Stockinette, and simple decorative stitches, resembling complex stitch patterns. Beautifully knitted fabrics are produced, by combining a variety of available yarns. Before pairing yarns together, consider the yarn content, color, and needle size. All these elements, in combination, will affect the final texture, and color of the knitted fabric.

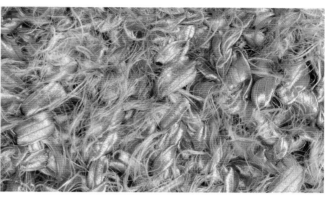

Feathery Textures

Light and airy knitted fabrics can be achieved with large needles, and fine yarns. With the Fringed Wrap, we mixed, two eyelash yarns, with a silky ribbon yarn. The idea was to create a gossamer-like fabric. By keeping the color range in the same

Surface Textures

To create a wonderful texture, combine bouclé yarn, with a bulky weight yarn, knit in a simple Stockinette stitch pattern. For example, The Chenille Ruffle Top is knit with a lush, deep purple, chenille yarn, and a contrasting blue, slubbed bouclé yarn. You don't see the thin strands of the bouclé, only the nubby yarn surrounded by velvety chenille fibers. If the top were knit with two yarns of a similar color, you could not appreciate the patterned surface texture. The result is a speckled surface pattern, resulting in a new textural combination.

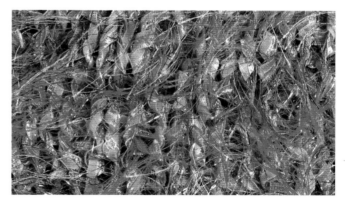

family of red/purple hues, we were able to add sparkle, by accenting them with two metallic, and iridescent eyelash yarns. The combined effect is a fringy open weave, delicate texture, that's perfect for wraps, and stoles.

When pairing yarns, consider yarn weight, color, and needle size to achieve beautiful combinations in the final knitted fabric.

Openwork Textures

Have you ever tried knitting a fur yarn in an openwork yarn over stitch pattern? In the Spring Sweater, we paired wide copper, flat ribbon yarn, with a colorful, feathery, wispy fur yarn in an openwork pattern. The result is a delicate airy texture that looks complex. The delicate fibers form a wonderful mesh that's intertwined with the metallic ribbon.

Beyond the Scarf Projects

Let's start our knitting adventure! As you progress through the book, your skills will advance with each project. We start off Easy, with a super-simple Fringed Wrap, cool Jazzy Belt, and Beaded Flip-flops.

The Beginner's Vintage Camisole, Chenille Ruffle Top, and Chenille Bag patterns are easy to knit with soft, chenille yarns; while the chic mini Ruffle Poncho is perfect on circular needles. Knit with the newest yarn, cool Jelly Yarn®, when making the Boa Jelly Purse, and Jelly Beach Bags.

Cruise to the Advanced Beginner projects beginning with a simple, short sleeved Spring Sweater. Learn to knit with beads while making the Beaded Handbag, and Lace Beaded Top. We have included a twin set project with the Cozy Capelet, and Easy Skirt ensemble. Finally, knit that basic black shrug to complete your fashion wardrobe. Don't forget to look for the yarn substitutions listed with every pattern.

We're ready to begin the knitting party that will fill your fashion closet with ruffled knitwear, beaded accessories, lacework tops, and embellished fashions. How about you?

❧ Fringed Wrap ❧

EASY

This off-the-shoulder tube wrap is an elegant accent for any outfit. Pair shimmering ribbon with two unique iridescent eyelash yarns for a sparkling, gossamer stole. The wrap is knit on large needles for a stretchable, comfy fit. Cast on, and bind off edges are self-fringing for a super-simple pattern. The soft knit flower, and beads are the perfect embellishment for that classic look.

Yarn

1 ball Trendsetter Yarns *Metal* 90yds (83m)
20g (100% polyester) Color: #15 Amethyst/Purple

1 ball Trendsetter Yarns *Aura* 90yds (83m)
20g (100% polyester) Color: #206 Cherry Multi

1 ball Katia *Chic Print* 70yds (59m)
50g (54% wool, 43% polyamide, 3% polyester) Color: #5750

1 ball Plymouth Yarn *Sinsation* 38yds (35m)
50g (80% rayon, 20% wool) Color: #3332

1 ball Trendsetter Yarns *Willow* 70yds (65m)
50g (100% polyester) Color: #20

Needles & Materials

One pair each of US #8 (5mm), US #19 (15mm) and
US #35 (19mm) needles or size needed to obtain gauge.

36–Cat's eye glass beads

Sizes

One size fits all.

Finished Measurements

36" (91cm) wide x 10" (25cm) long.

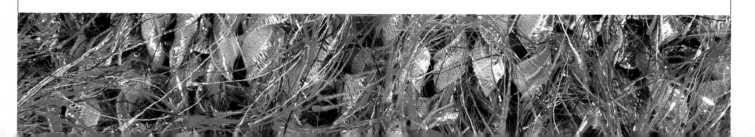

GAUGE

In Stockinette stitch pattern, 5 sts and 11 rows = 4" (10cm) with size US #35 needles.

STOCKINETTE STITCH PATTERN

Row 1: K across.

Row 2: P across.

Repeat rows 1 and 2.

SUBSTITUTION YARNS

Trendsetter Yarns *Metal* = Any eyelash yarn

Trendsetter Yarns *Aura* = Any eyelash yarn

Katia *Chic Print* = Lion Brand Yarn *Incredible*

Plymouth Yarn *Sinsation* = Lion Brand Yarn *Chenille Thick & Quick*

Trendsetter Yarns *Willow* = Lion Brand Yarn *Fun Fur*

NOTES

* After rows 1 and 18, comb fibers downward on needle.

* When using US #35 needles, straighten stitches after each row.

* Push *Sinsation* yarn through glass beads with the pointed end of a tapestry needle.

Fringed Wrap Pattern

Front and Back (one piece)

With US #19 needles working 2 strands of *Willow* and 1 strand each of *Metal* and *Aura* held tog, CO 48 sts.

Row 1: K across.

Row 2: Change to US #35 needles, add 1 strand of *Chic Print* yarn and K across.

Row 3: Drop 2 strands of *Willow*, Purl across.

Rows 4–17: Beginning with K row, work in St st for 14 rows.

Row 18: Join 2 strands of *Willow*, K across.

Row 19: Change to US #19 needles, drop *Chic Print* and K across.

Row 20: K across.

Row 21: K across.

Row 22: BO loosely with US #35 needle.

Knit Flower

Working 1 strand of *Sinsation* yarn, starting from 60" from tail end, CO 60 sts with US #8 needles.

Straighten stitches on needle as needed.

Row 1: K across.

Row 2: P across.

Row 3: K across.

Row 4: P across.

Row 5: K2tog across the row.

BO.

Beginning with the BO end, wrap the piece around the center several times to form the flower. Sew together with invisible thread.

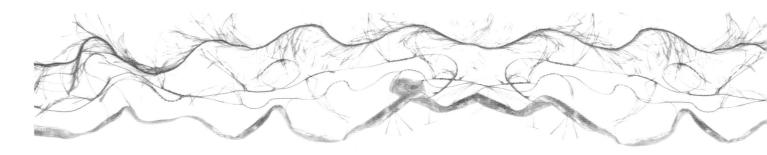

Finishing

Sew side seams with *Chic Print* yarn to create tube wrap. Cut two 6" (15cm) strands of *Chic Print* yarn. With wrong side out, position wrap on a flat surface with seam in the center. Tie the cut strands around the center of the seam with a tight knot and trim ends.

Turn right side out and sew flower to ruched center. Cut three 5" (12.5cm) strands each of *Chic Print* and *Sinsation* yarns. Thread 3 glass beads on each end and tie a knot. Fold strands in half and trim ends. Gather folded strands, tie a 6" (15cm) piece of *Sinsation* yarn through the folded loops and make a knot. Wind *Sinsation* yarn around the flower, with beaded strands hanging at the bottom. Tie a secure knot in place at the top of the flower. Trim ends.

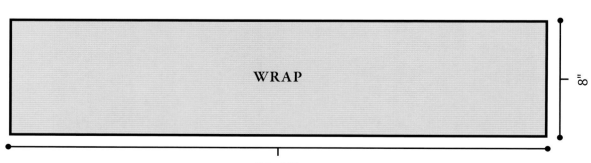

WRAP

8"

36–42"

Jazzy Belt

EASY

Accessories are an important part of every wardrobe. Our jazzy belt, knit with glossy black licorice Jelly Yarn, *adds that finishing touch. Slick and irresistible, this look-at-me embellishment features a novel knit-on-buckle technique with a decorative selvage edge. Create your own mix with 7 delicious colors to match your outfits.*

Yarn

2 balls Yummy Yarns® Fine *Jelly Yarn*® 85yds (78m)
200g (100% vinyl) Color: Back Licorice

Needles & Materials

US #6 (4.00 mm) needles or size needed to obtain gauge.
1 Prym Dritz square belt buckle

Sizes

S-M (L-XL) Instructions are for smallest size,
with changes for other sizes in parentheses.

Finished Measurements

1.5" (4cm) wide x 36–38 (40–42)"/
91–96.5 (101.5–106.5)cm long.

GAUGE

In Garter stitch pattern, 20 sts and 32 rows = 4" (10cm).

GARTER STITCH PATTERN

Knit every row.

SUBSTITUTION YARNS

Replace Yummy Yarns® Fine *Jelly Yarn*® with Colors: Hot Pink Candy, Raspberry Sorbet, Orange Sherbet, Blue Taffy, Pink Parfait, and Lemon-Lime Ice.

NOTES

* Pull yarn from center of each ball at the same time, and keep separated to prevent tangling.

* Tie a secure knot with *Jelly Yarn*® by pulling strands until they stretch, then release.

* Use Armor All® to help stitches glide on the needle.

Jazzy Belt Pattern

Belt

This method knits the belt neatly onto the buckle.

For alternate method of sewing buckle onto finished belt, CO 6 sts and skip to Row 3. See *Attaching the Buckle at end of pattern.

With 2 strands of FINE *Jelly Yarn*® held tog, make a slip knot and CO 1 st. Make sure you have about 12 inches (30.5cm) of tail yarn. Position the buckle with the wrong side up. Loop the tail up and over the buckle horizontal pin, shown in the photo. Keep the yarn to the back of the needle.

Pull the needle up close to the horizontal pin, to keep the loop taut.

Make the 2nd CO stitch. Once the 2nd CO stitch is made, pull all the strands taut. Again, loop the tail end up and over the horizontal buckle pin. Keep the yarn to the back of the needle, pull all the strands taut.

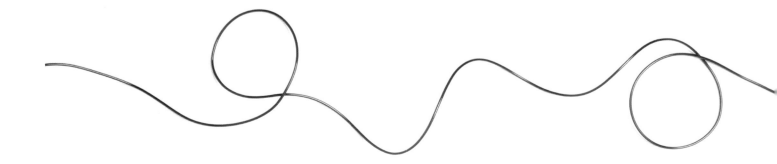

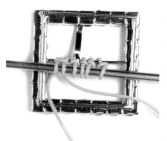

Repeat steps #1 and #2 until you have 6 CO stitches. After the 3rd cast on stitch, wrap the loop before the prong. Then make the 4th CO st and wrap, 5th CO st and wrap, and 6th CO st and wrap after the prong. After you make the 6th cast on stitch wrap the yarn around the horizontal pin and make a tight knot. Stretch the yarn so the knot holds, then release, and make another tight knot.

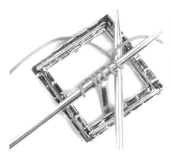

Rows 1–2: To make the 1st knit row, insert the needle into the 1st stitch as shown in the photo.

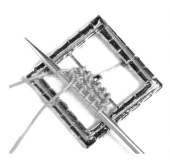

Gently knit the stitch and slip onto the right-hand needle. It might be difficult to make this 1st stitch because the needle is against the buckle, but pull the yarn tightly so it doesn't fall off. Once you do this row, the rest of the row is easier.

Row 3: Bring yarn forward as if to Purl, Slip 1st stitch onto right needle, and bring yarn back to knit position. Knit across.

Repeat Row 3 for desired length of belt 36–38 (40–42)"/ 91–96.5 (101.5–106.5)cm. Leave 6" (15cm) of overlap around waist or hips.

Next Row: Bring yarn forward as if to Purl, Slip 1st stitch onto right needle, and bring yarn back to knit position. K2tog, K2tog, Knit 1 = 4 sts.

Last Row: Bring yarn forward as if to Purl, Slip 1st stitch onto right needle, and bring yarn back to knit position. K2tog, Knit 1 = 3 sts.

BO last 3 stitches loosely.

*Attaching the Buckle—*Alternate method of attaching buckle to knitted belt.*

Make sure the tong is centered on the right side of the buckle. With the tail end of the yarn, tie the buckle bar to the cast on edge with a very tight double knot. Use a tapestry needle to sew the cast on edge to the buckle, wrapping around the bar each time. Sew equally on both sides of the centered tong.

BELT	1.25"

36 (38, 40, 42)"

∞ Beaded Flip-flops ∞

EASY

Fashion flip-flops are a must. Knit them with high-gloss, water-resistant Jelly Yarn® in a super-easy Garter stitch pattern, and a unique cast on wrap technique. Shimmering glass beads add pizzazz and sparkle. Both contemporary and comfortable, you'll enjoy them on the beach or on the town.

Yarn

2 balls Yummy Yarns® Fine *Jelly Yarn*® 85yds (78m)
200g (100% vinyl) Color: Lemon-Lime Ice

Needles & Materials

US #5 (3.75mm) needles or size needed to obtain gauge.

90–Size E glass beads

1 Rhinestone pin

1 Pair Flip-flops

Finished Measurements

.75" (2cm) wide x 4" (10cm) long.

GAUGE

In Garter stitch pattern, 15 sts and 37 rows = 4" (10cm) with 1 beaded strand of *Jelly Yarn*®.

GARTER STITCH PATTERN

Knit every row.

SUBSTITUTION YARNS

Replace Yummy Yarns® Fine *Jelly Yarn*® with Colors: Hot Pink Candy, Raspberry Sorbet, Orange Sherbet, Blue Taffy, Pink Parfait, or Black Licorice.

NOTES

✳ Use Armor All® to help stitches glide on the needle.

✳ Tie a secure knot with *Jelly Yarn*® by pulling strands until they stretch, then release.

✳ Make sure beads are on the right side. If bead slips through to wrong side, push through knitting to right side.

Beaded Flip-flops Pattern

Right Strap (one piece)

The cast on wrap technique is a cool way to knit directly onto the Flip-flop strap. If you prefer to sew the knitted pieces onto the Flip-flop straps, skip the cast on wrap technique, string 45 beads on Fine *Jelly Yarn*® and proceed to Row 1. *See, "Attaching Knitted Pieces to Flip-flops," below.

Cast On Wrap Technique

String 45 beads on Fine *Jelly Yarn*®.

Start at lower end (heel) on the right strap. Begin with 72" (183cm) from the ball yarn.

Align needle to outer edge of strap and CO 1 st. Wrap the yarn around the strap from the outside to the inside, and BEHIND the needle.

Repeat from * to * until there are 15 CO sts, and 15 wraps around the Flip-flop strap.

Tie a tight knot with the tail end and ball strand.

Row 1: K across.

Row 2: *Place 1 bead, positioned in the back of the needle, K1, * repeat from * to * across row.

Row 3: K across.

Row 4: *Place 1 bead, positioned in the back of the needle, K1, * repeat from * to * across row.

Row 5: K across.

Row 6: *Place 1 bead, positioned in the back of the needle, K1, * repeat from * to * across row.

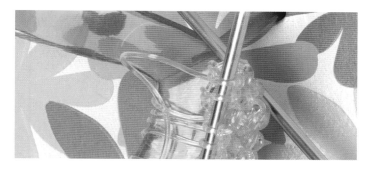

Row 7: Cut 72" (183cm) from ball yarn. K1, *weave end of yarn through 1st loop on wrapped strap, K1. * Repeat from * to * across row through all the wrapped loops on the strap. This row will make the knitted piece fit securely on top of the strap.

BO and tie a tight knot with the yarn strands. Weave ends under strap and trim.

Left Strap (one piece)

Knit as for Right Strap but begin CO at upper end (toe) left strap.

*Attaching Knitted Pieces to Flip-flops

(Use this method to attach, if you are NOT using cast on wrap technique)

Straighten beaded knit piece. Using the yarn tail, wrap around the entire length of the flip-flop strap, and tie knot securely underneath. Weave ends under strap and trim.

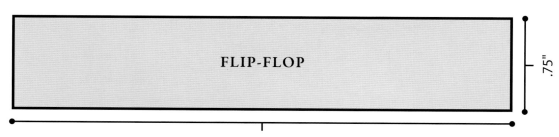

FLIP-FLOP

.75"

4"

Vintage Camisole

BEGINNER

Treat yourself to a lush camisole top! Knit this sinfully soft chenille yarn with two classic shades, in an easy vintage design. We chose burgundy yarn for the edging, and straps, and warm coral for the bodice. The plush texture feels incredibly soft against the skin. Add a dazzling rhinestone pin for a vintage look.

Yarn

3 (4, 5, 6, 7) balls Plymouth Yarn *Sinsation* 38yds (35m)
50g (80% rayon, 20% wool) Color: #3326

2 (2, 2, 3, 4) balls Plymouth Yarn *Sinsation* 38yds (35m)
50g (80% rayon, 20% wool) Color: #3369

Needles & Materials

One pair each of US #13 (9mm) and
US #10.5 (6.50mm) needles or size needed to obtain gauge.

1 Vintage pin

Sizes

XS (S, M, L, XL) Instructions are for smallest size,
with changes for other sizes in parentheses.

Finished Measurements

Chest: 34 (36, 38, 40, 42)"/86 (91, 96.5, 101.5, 107)cm.
Length: 12 (13, 14, 15, 16)"/30.5 (33, 35.5, 38, 40.5)cm.

GAUGE

In Stockinette stitch pattern, 13 sts and 18 rows = 4" (10cm) with US #10.5 needles.

STOCKINETTE STITCH PATTERN

Row 1: K across.

Row 2: P across.

Repeat rows 1 and 2.

SUBSTITUTION YARNS

Plymouth Yarn *Sinsation* = Berroco *Chinchilla Bulky*

NOTES

* For best results, use a large rhinestone or cameo pin.

* If you are using different color yarns then specified in the pattern, choose 2 different shades of the same color.

* Instead of a pin, tie ribbon strands around center of bust.

Vintage Camisole Pattern

Front and Back (two pieces)

Bodice

With US #13 needles using *Sinsation* Color: 3369 (burgundy), CO 40 (42, 44, 46, 48) sts.

Row 1: K across the row.

Row 2: Change to *Sinsation* Color: 3326 (coral) and P across row.

Row 3: Beginning with knit row, work in St st for 7.5 (8.5, 9, 9.5, 10)"/19 (21.5, 23, 24, 25)cm ending in Purl row.

Next Row: Change to *Sinsation* Color: 3369, and K across the row.

Next Row: K across the row.

Next Row: P across the row.

Next Row: K across the row.

Next Row: P across the row.

Next Row: Change to US #10.5 needles using *Sinsation* Color: 3326 and K1, Inc 15 (16, 16, 18, 19) sts across the row = 55 (58, 60, 64, 67) sts.

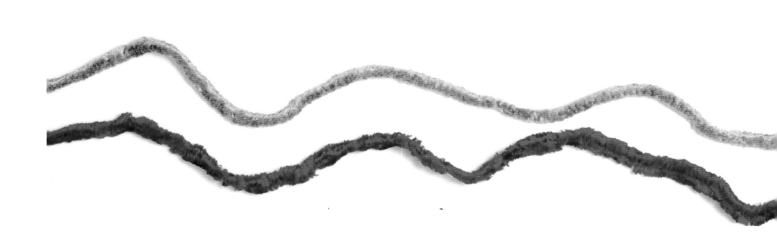

Bust

Work in St st for a total of 4.5 (4.5, 5, 5.5, 6)"/11 (11, 13, 14, 15)cm ending in a Purl row.

Change to *Sinsation* Color: 3369 and K across the next 3 rows.

Neckline and Shoulder Straps

BO 12 sts, K4 (place sts on a stitch holder), BO 23 (26, 28, 32, 35) sts, K4, BO 12 sts.

Knit shoulder straps individually in St st for 5 (5, 6, 6, 7)"/13 (13,15,15, 17.5)cm.

BO loosely.

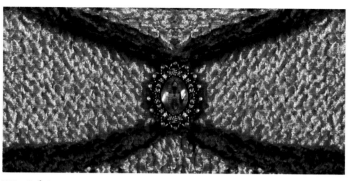

Finishing

Sew shoulders together. Position and sew side seams. Pinch neckline, and bottom of bustline border together with rhinestone or cameo pin.

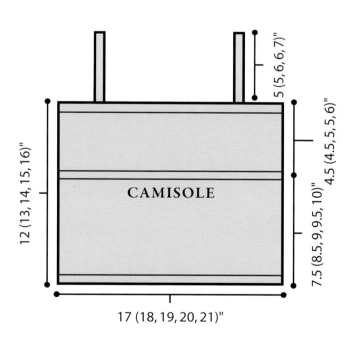

CAMISOLE

5 (5, 6, 6, 7)"

4.5 (4.5, 5, 5, 6)"

12 (13, 14, 15, 16)"

7.5 (8.5, 9, 9.5, 10)"

17 (18, 19, 20, 21)"

❦ Ruffle Poncho ❦

BEGINNER

Mini-ponchos are hot! Spice-up your outfits with this silky-soft, ruffle cover-up. Knit it with velvety soft ribbon yarn on circular needles. You'll like the lightweight comfy fit and dazzling ruffle edge. Invigorate your look with this chic mini that tells everyone you've come to party.

Yarn

3 (4) balls Katia *Chic Print* 70yds (59m)
50g (54% wool, 43% polyamide, 3% polyester) Color: #5750

3 (4) balls GGH *Milano* 86yds (80m)
50g (40% nylon, 30% acrylic, 30% new wool) Color: #005

Needles & Materials

US #19 (15mm) 29" (73.5cm) circular needles
or size needed to obtain gauge.

Sizes

S-M (L-XL) Instructions are for smallest size,
with changes for other sizes in parentheses.

Finished Measurements

36–38 (40–42)"/91–96 (101.5, 106.5)cm wide x 9" (25cm) long.

GAUGE

In Yarn Over stitch pattern, 8 sts and 5 rows = 4"
(10cm) excluding ruffled edge

YARN OVER STITCH PATTERN

YO, K2tog repeat from * to * across row.

SUBSTITUTION YARNS

Katia *Chic Print* = Lion Brand Yarn *Incredible*

GGH *Milano* = Berroco *Gem*

NOTES

✻ Make sure stitches are straight on cast on row
before joining.

✻ Be sure to use 2 different color stitch markers.

✻ For a fringed look, include an eyelash yarn held
together with the *Chic Print,* and *Milano* yarns.

Ruffle Poncho Pattern

Poncho (one piece)

With circular needles, working 1 strand each of *Chic Print*
and *Milano* held tog, CO 66 (72) sts.

Join in the round and place stitch marker.

Rnd 1: K round.

Rnd 2: P round.

Rnd 3: *YO, K2tog* repeat from * to * across row to
33rd st, place different color stitch marker,

YO, K2tog repeat from * to end of round.

Rnd 4: K round.

Rnd 5: Inc 1, Inc 1, *YO, K2tog* repeat from * to * across
row to stitch marker, Inc 1, Inc 1, *YO, K2tog* repeat
from * to end of round = 70 (76) stitches.

Rnd 6: K round.

Rnd 7: Inc 1, Inc 1, *YO, K2tog* repeat from * to * across
row to stitch marker, Inc 1, Inc 1, *YO, K2tog* repeat
from * to end of round = 74 (80) stitches.

Rnd 8: K round.

Rnd 9: Inc 1, Inc 1, *YO, K2tog* repeat from * to * across
row to stitch marker, Inc 1, Inc 1, *YO, K2tog* repeat
from * to end of round = 78 (84) stitches.

Rnd 10: K round.

Rnd 11: *YO, K2tog* repeat from * to * across row.

Rnd 12: K round.

Rnd 13: *YO, K2tog* repeat from * to * across row.

Rnd 14: K round.

Rnd 15: *YO, K2tog* repeat from * to * across row.

Rnd 16: K round.

Rnd 17: *YO, K2tog* repeat from * to * across row.

Rnd 18: K round.

Rnd 19: *YO, K2tog* repeat from * to * across row.

Rnd 20: K round.

Rnd 21: *YO, K2tog* repeat from * to * across row.

Rnd 22: K round.

Rnd 23: *YO, K2tog* repeat from * to * across row.

Rnd 24: K round.

Rnd 25: *YO, K2tog* repeat from * to * across row.

Rnd 26: K round.

Rnd 27: *YO, K2tog* repeat from * to * across row.

Rnd 28: K round.

Rnd 29: *YO, K2tog* repeat from * to * across row.

Rnd 30: K round.

Rnd 31: Inc every st = 156 sts.

Rnd 32: K round.

Rnd 33: Inc every st = 312 sts.

Rnd 34: P round.

Rnd 35: BO loosely.

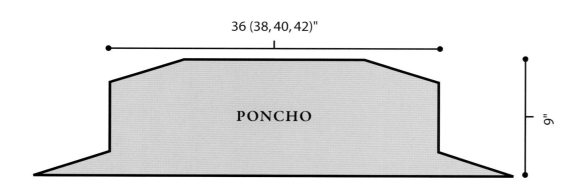

36 (38, 40, 42)"

PONCHO

9"

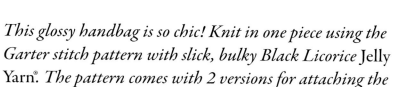

Boa Jelly Purse

BEGINNER

This glossy handbag is so chic! Knit in one piece using the Garter stitch pattern with slick, bulky Black Licorice Jelly Yarn®. The pattern comes with 2 versions for attaching the handles. Sew two side seams for quick assembly, and add a red and black marabou boa for an easy stylish finish!

Yarn

2 balls Yummy Yarns® Bulky *Jelly Yarn*® 85yds (78m)
240g (100% vinyl) Color: Black Licorice

Needles & Materials

US #13 (9mm) METAL needles or size needed to obtain gauge.
2 Prym Dritz Bag Boutique black twist purse handles #9884
2.5" (6cm) Marabou feather boa
Crochet hook

Finished Measurements

12" (30.5cm) wide x 9" (23cm) long.

GAUGE

In Garter stitch pattern, 10 sts and 18 rows = 4" (10cm) with 2 strands of Bulky *Jelly Yarn*® held tog.

GARTER STITCH PATTERN

Knit every row.

SUBSTITUTION YARNS

Replace Yummy Yarns® Bulky *Jelly Yarn*® with Colors: Hot Pink Candy, Raspberry Sorbet, Orange Sherbet, Blue Taffy, Pink Parfait and Lemon-Lime Ice.

NOTES

❋ Pull yarn from center of each ball at the same time, and keep separated to prevent tangling.

❋ Tie a secure knot with *Jelly Yarn*® by pulling strands until they stretch, then release.

❋ Use Armor All® to help stitches glide on the needle.

Boa Jelly Purse Pattern

Cast on Versions

There are two versions for casting on. With Version 1, cast on onto the needle and handle together. With Version 2, knit the purse, and sewn on the handle when you are finished knitting.

Version 1: Handle Cast On Technique With 1st Handle (see page 19)

This is a good method for securing the purse handles to the knitting. See page 19, how to cast on, and knit the handles together. After the handle is cast on, proceed to row 1.

Version 2: Regular CO (attach handles when finished)

CO 23 sts with 2 strands held tog and proceed to row 1.

Front and Back (one piece)

With 2 strands from the tail end, tie a very tight knot after last CO st, leaving about 15" (38cm) of CO strands for sewing side seams later.

Rows 1–16: K across.

Row 17: K1, Inc 1 st, K across to last 2 sts, Inc 1 st, K1 = 25 sts.

Row 18: K across.

Row 19: K1, Inc 1 st, K across to last 2 sts, Inc 1 st, K1 = 27 sts.

Row 20: K across.

Row 21: K1, Inc 1 st, K across to last 2 sts, Inc 1 st, K1 = 29 sts.

Row 22: K across.

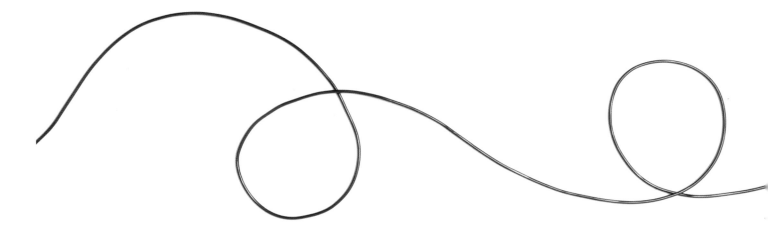

Row 23: K across.

Row 24: (RS) P across. (This will make a curve in your knitting to form the bottom of the purse.)

Row 25: K across.

Row 26: P across.

Row 27: K across.

Row 28: K across.

Row 29: K1, K2tog, K across to last 3 sts, K2tog, K1 = 27 sts.

Row 30: K across.

Row 31: K1, K2tog, K across to last 3 sts, K2tog, K1 = 25 sts.

Row 32: K across.

Row 33: K1, K2tog, K across to last 3 sts, K2tog, K1 = 23 sts.

Rows 34–41: K across.

Version 1: Finishing

Handle Bind Off Technique With 2nd Handle (see page 19)

Row 42: See page 19, how to knit 2nd handle onto purse.

Row 43: Fold handle flat on inside of purse and BO loosely. Leave long strands for sewing side seams.

Sew side seams with remaining double strand bind off, and cast on tails held tog. Using monofilament thread, sew boa around edge of purse twice using a wrap stitch, making sure to insert needle through core of boa. Tuck end in, and sew securely.

Version 2: Attaching Handles and Finishing

Without Handles

Row 42: K across row.

Row 43: BO loosely. Leave long strands for sewing side seams.

Position 1st handle centered along cast on edge. With 1 strand of *Jelly Yarn®* and crochet hook, loop through cast on edge and through hole opening of purse handle. Make a very tight knot. Repeat 3 times. Attach other end of

purse handle. Repeat on bind off edge with 2nd handle. Sew side seams with remaining double strand bind off and cast on tails held tog. Using monofilament thread, sew boa around edge of purse twice using a wrap stitch, making sure to insert needle through core of boa. Tuck end in, and sew securely.

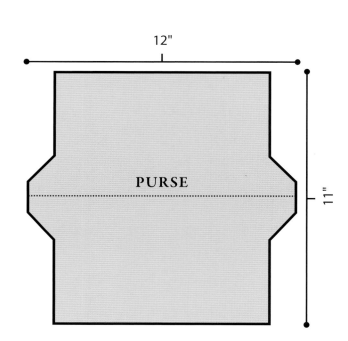

12"

PURSE

11"

Jelly Beach Bags

BEGINNER AND EASY

Beach bags are a must-have accessory for a fun afternoon at the seashore. Knit one with glossy, vinyl Jelly Yarn®, the coolest yarn in your knitting bag. This stretchable, quick-knit bag uses circular needles with an easy yarn over pattern. It doubles as a roomy market bag for all the essentials. Knit a cute, Mini-jelly bag variation too!

Yarn

2 balls Yummy Yarns® Fine *Jelly Yarn®* 85yds (78m)
200g (100% vinyl) Color: Hot Pink Candy

2 balls Yummy Yarns® Bulky *Jelly Yarn®* 65yds (60m)
240g (100% vinyl) Color: Lemon-Lime Ice

Needles & Materials

One pair each of US #19 (15mm) 29" (73.5cm) circular and
US #19 (15mm) straight needles or size needed to obtain gauge.

2 Round bamboo handles

2 Round black plastic handles

Finished Measurements

Jelly Beach Bag 13" (33cm) wide x 10" (25cm) long.
Mini-jelly Bag 10" (25cm) wide x 9" (23cm) long.

GAUGE

Jelly Beach Bag in Yarn Over stitch pattern, 9 sts and 10 rows = 4" (10cm).

Mini-jelly Bag in Garter stitch pattern, 8 sts and 11 rows = 4" (10cm).

YARN OVER STITCH PATTERN

YO, K2tog repeat from * to * across row.

GARTER STITCH PATTERN

Knit every row.

SUBSTITUTION YARNS

Replace Yummy Yarns® Fine Hot Pink Candy *Jelly Yarn*® with Colors: Raspberry Sorbet, Orange Sherbet, Blue Taffy, Pink Parfait, and Lemon-Lime Ice.

NOTES

✳ Pull and straighten *Jelly Yarn*® stitches after each row.

✳ Knitted texture will be curly, but will stretch and expand once filled.

✳ Use Armor All® to help stitches glide on the needle.

Jelly Beach Bag Pattern

Bag (one piece)

The pattern will seem wider than longer. The bag will stretch out when in use.

Use Armor All® to help stitches glide on the needle.

Using circular needles and 1 strand of Fine *Jelly Yarn*®, CO 60 sts.

Join in the round and place stitch marker.

Rnd 1: K around.

Rnd 2: *YO, K2tog* repeat from * to * across row.

Repeat rows 1 and 2 for 10" (25cm).

BO.

Attaching Purse to Round Handles

Cut 18" (46cm) of double stranded Fine *Jelly Yarn*® from ball. On the 8th stitch along the cast on edge, tie a secure knot with the strands, pull tightly until the yarn stretches, then release.

Pull *Jelly Yarn*® double strands through the 9th cast on stitch, loop with crochet hook, and wrap around one purse handle. Make taut. Repeat along edge, every 3 stitches to the 51st stitch. Tie a secure knot with the strand ends. Repeat for other side.

Mini-Jelly Bag Pattern

Mini Bag (one piece)

The bag stretches out when in use. Stretch out bag as you knit.

With US #15 straight needles and 1 strand of Bulky *Jelly Yarn*®, CO 15 sts.

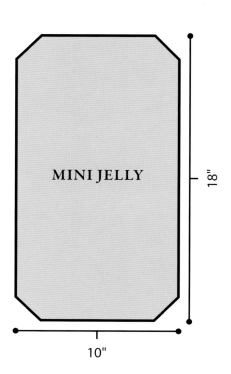

Row 1: K across.

Row 2: K across.

Row 3: K across.

Row 4: K2, Inc 1, K across to last 3 sts, Inc 1, K2 = 17 sts

Row 5: K across.

Row 6: K2, Inc 1, K across to last 3 sts, Inc 1, K2 = 19 sts

Rows 7–57: K across every row.

Row 58: K2, K2tog, K across to last 4 sts, K2tog, K2 = 17 sts

Row 59: K across.

Row 60: K across.

Row 61: K across.

Row 62: K across.

BO loosely.

Finishing and Attaching Purse to Round Handles

Sew side seams with 2 strands of Bulky *Jelly Yarn*® leaving about 2" (5cm) from cast on edge.

Cut two 15" (30.5cm) strands Bulky *Jelly Yarn*® and tie a secure knot to the bag with the strands, pull tightly until the yarn stretches, then release. With a crochet hook, pull the 2 strands of *Jelly Yarn*® through the 1st cast on stitch and wrap around the round handle from the inside to the outside and through the 2nd stitch.

Repeat across the row.

Repeat for the second handle except work the strands through the bind off row.

Tie a secure tight knot with the strand ends.

BEACH BAG

10"

13"

MINI JELLY

18"

10"

Chenille Bag

BEGINNER

Knit this gorgeous purse with super-lush chenille yarn. Use the unique handle wrap technique for a smart design. Working in a Stockinette stitch pattern, knit the bag as a one-piece rectangle. Sew the side seams, embellish with beaded trim and a flower pendant—a real classic!

Yarn

2 balls Plymouth Yarn *Sinsation* 38yds (35m)
50g (80% rayon, 20% wool) Color: #3332

Needles & Materials

US #10.5 (6.50mm) needles or size needed to obtain gauge.
2 Prym Dritz triangular shaped black plastic purse handles #9898
1 yd (91.5cm) Beaded trim
2 Pure Allure flower pendants.

Finished Measurements

10" (25cm) wide x 6.5" (16.5cm) long.

GAUGE

In Stockinette stitch pattern, 16 sts and 18 rows = 4" (10cm).

STOCKINETTE STITCH PATTERN

Row 1: K across.

Row 2: P across.

Repeat rows 1 and 2.

SUBSTITUTION YARNS

Plymouth Yarn *Sinsation* = Berroco *Chinchilla Bulky*

NOTES

✳ Add 8" (20cm) of yarn to cast on, to sew side seams.

✳ Leave 8" (20cm) of yarn after bind off to sew side seams.

✳ Sew seams of bag wrong side out.

Chenille Bag Pattern

Cast On Handle Wrap Technique 1st Handle

This unique method secures the purse handles to the knitting, and creates a beautiful finished edge.

Begin 120" (305cm) from the tail end of the yarn. Loop ball end of yarn around your thumb, and CO 1 st using the Long Tail Cast On method.

Step 1: Align needle and purse handle side by side. Using tail end, wrap yarn from the back to the front around the handle, and position yarn BEHIND the needle.

Step 2: CO 2nd stitch. Using tail end, wrap yarn from the back to the front around the handle and position yarn between the handle and the needle.

Repeat until you have a total of 34 CO and wrapped stitches. Make CO stitches snug, but not too tight.

Front and Back (one piece)

The handle is now attached to your knitting. When you knit across the first row, the knitting may feel a bit tight and will slide on the handle. This is typical. After the 1st row, slide stitches to the center on widest part of the handle.

Row 1: K across.

Row 2: P across.

Row 3: K1 st, Inc 1 st, K across to the last 2 sts, Inc 1 st, K1 st = 36 sts.

Row 4: P across.

Row 5: K1 st, Inc 1 st, K across to the last 2 sts, Inc 1 st, K1 st = 38 sts.

Row 6: P across.

Row 7: K1 st, Inc 1 st, K across to the last 2 sts, Inc 1 st, K1 st = 40 sts.

Rows 8–48: Work in St st.

Row 49: K across.

Row 50: P across.

Row 51: K1 st, K2tog, K across to the last 3 sts, K2tog, K1 st = 38 sts.

Row 52: P across.

Row 53: K1 st, K2tog, K across to the last 3 sts, K2tog, K1 st = 36 sts.

Row 54: P across.

Row 55: K across.

Cast On Handle Wrap Technique 2nd Handle

Finish the purse with this handle wrap technique. Cut 120" (305cm) from the yarn ball end.

Row 56: (WS) Align needle and purse handle side by side. *Using tail end, wrap yarn from the back to the front around the handle, and position yarn BEHIND the needle. Bring yarn forward, and P1, then bring yarn back between the needles.* Repeat from * to * across the row. Make stitches snug, but not too tight.

Fold handle against outside of purse and BO. Use remaining yarn to sew side seams.

Finishing

Sew side seams with *Sinsation* yarn.

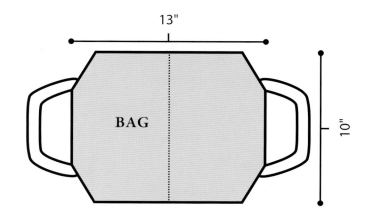

13"

BAG

10"

Chenille Ruffle Top

BEGINNER

Cuddly and stylish, this ruffle top is knit with soft chenille and cotton bouclé yarn. Create a beautiful textural pattern by combining the two yarns. This vibrant purple shell is worked in a Stockinette stitch pattern that allows for easy assembly. The feminine ruffle is knit separately with a cuddly-soft chenille yarn. Simple, yet chic!

Yarn

4 (4, 5, 5) balls Maggi Knits *Maggi's Cotton* 77yds (71m)
50g (70% cotton, 30% viscose) Color: #03

4 (4, 5, 5) balls Plymouth Yarn *Sinsation* 38yds (35m)
50g (80% rayon, 20% wool) Color: #3381

Needles & Materials

One pair each of US #10.5 (6.5mm), US #11 (8mm),
and US #13 (9mm) needles or size needed to obtain gauge.

Sizes

S (M, L, XL) Instructions are for smallest size,
with changes for other sizes in parentheses.

Finished Measurements

Chest: 34 (36, 38, 40)"/86 (91, 96.5, 101.5)cm.
Total Length: 18 (18.5, 19, 19.5)"/45.5 (47, 48, 49.5)cm.

GAUGE

In Stockinette stitch pattern, 10 sts and 10 rows = 4" (10cm).

SEED STITCH PATTERN

Row 1: K1, P1 across the row, ending in K1.

Repeat this row.

STOCKINETTE STITCH PATTERN

Row 1: K across.

Row 2: P across.

Repeat rows 1 and 2.

SUBSTITUTION YARNS

Maggi Knits *Maggi's Cotton* = Debbie Bliss *Cashmerino Astrakhan*

Plymouth Yarn *Sinsation* = Berroco *Chinchilla Bulky*

NOTES

✳ Sew beaded trim along ruffle neckline for embellished edge.

✳ If the Seed stitch pattern is too difficult, you can replace the first 4 rows of the Front and Back, with the Garter stitch pattern.

✳ Hand wash only. Lay flat to dry.

Chenille Ruffle Top Pattern

Back (one piece)

With US #11 needles using 1 strand of *Sinsation*, CO 43 (45, 47, 51) sts.

Rows 1–4: Work in Seed stitch pattern.

Change to US #13 needles using 1 strand each of *Maggi's Cotton* and *Sinsation* held tog.

Row 5: (RS) K across the row.

Row 6: K1, P across the row, ending K1.

Rep rows 5 and 6 until piece measures 11 (11, 12, 12)"/ 28 (28, 30.5, 30.5)cm from beginning, ending on a Purl row.

Armholes

(RS) BO the first 2 sts, K across the row = 41 (43, 45, 49) sts

BO the first 2 sts, P across the row = 39 (41, 43, 47) sts

Next Row: K2, K2tog, K across to last 4 sts, (Sl1, K1, PSSO) K2 = 37 (39, 41, 45) sts

Next Row: K1, P across, ending K1.

Repeat last 2 rows three more times = 31 (33, 35, 39) sts

Neckline and Shoulders

Work both sides at once with separate balls of yarn.

Next Row: K7 (8, 9, 11) BO 17 sts, K7 (8, 9, 11)

Next Row: P7 (8, 9, 11) remaining sts each side.

Next Row: K across, dec 1 st each neck edge once.

Next Row: P6 (7, 8, 10) remaining sts each side.

Next Row: K across, dec 1 st each neck edge once =
5 (6, 7, 8) sts remaining each side.

Continue in St st until piece measures18 (18.5, 19,
19.5)"/45.5 (47, 48, 49.5)cm from beginning, ending
on a Purl row.

BO loosely.

Front (one piece)

Work same as for back.

Ruffle

With US #10.5 needles using 1 strand of *Sinsation*,
CO 120 (126, 133, 140) sts.

Rows 1–2: Work in Garter stitch pattern.

Row 3: Beg on (WS) and work in St st until piece
measures 3" (7.5)cm.

Next row: K 0 (2, 1, 0), *K1, K3tog; rep from * across
the row = 60 (64, 67, 70) sts.

BO loosely.

Finishing

Lay flat and position (RS) of ruffle edge and (WS) of
front neckline, and sew together. Position shoulders
and side seams together, and sew with *Sinsation* yarn
using the Mattress Stitch.

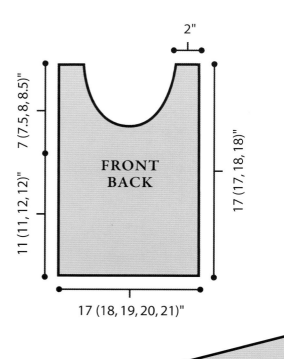

Spring Sweater

ADVANCED BEGINNER

This short sleeved, copper color sweater is a chic, one-of-a-kind style. The top is created from a unique mix of ribbon and soft fur yarn. Worked in a Stockinette stitch pattern, the openwork yarn over for the sleeves, highlights the metallic wide ribbon yarn. Simply stunning!

Yarn

4 (5, 6, 7, 8) balls Plymouth Yarn *Jungle* 61yds (56m)
50g (100% nylon) Color: #733

2 (3, 3, 3, 4) balls Trendsetter Yarns *Viola* 180yds (166m)
50g (100% nylon) Color: #17

Needles & Materials

US #17 (12.75mm) needles or size needed to obtain gauge.

1–1.5" (4cm) Diameter button

Sizes

XS (S, M, L, XL) Instructions are for smallest size,
with changes for other sizes in parentheses.

Finished Measurements

Chest: 34 (36, 38, 40, 42)"/86 (91, 96.5, 101.5, 106.5)cm.
Total Length: 15.5 (16, 16.5, 17, 18)"/39 (40.5, 42, 43, 46)cm.

GAUGE

In Stockinette stitch pattern, 10 sts and 13 rows = 4" (10cm).

GARTER STITCH PATTERN

Knit every row.

STOCKINETTE STITCH PATTERN

Row 1: K across.

Row 2: P across.

Repeat rows 1 and 2.

SUBSTITUTION YARNS

Plymouth Yarn *Jungle* = Lion Brand Yarn *Incredible*

Trendsetter Yarns *Viola* = Lion Brand Yarn *Tiffany* or Crystal Palace Yarns *Whisper*

NOTES

❊ If you want less fur texture, work the *Viola* yarn every knit row.

❊ If the Seed stitch pattern is too difficult, you can replace the first 4 rows of the Front and Back, with the Garter stitch pattern.

❊ For best results, comb fur with a fine toothed-comb.

Spring Sweater Pattern

Back

With 1 strand of *Jungle*, CO 42 (45, 47, 50, 52) sts.

Rows 1–3: Work in Garter stitch pattern.

Continue in St st until piece measures 15.5 (16, 16.5, 17, 18)"/39 (40.5, 42, 43, 46)cm.

End on a Purl row.

BO loosely.

Right Front

With 1 strand of *Jungle*, CO 21 (22, 24, 25, 26) sts.

Rows 1–3: Work in Garter stitch pattern.

Row 4: K across.

Row 5: Join 1 strand of *Viola* yarn and P across the row.

Row 6: (To make button hole) K2 (YO, K2tog) K across the row.

Rows 7–27: Beginning with a K row, work in St st stitch for 21 rows.

Row 28: K2, (Sl1, K1, PSSO) K across = 20 (21, 23, 24, 25) sts.

Row 29: BO 2 sts, P across the row =18 (19, 21, 22, 23) sts.

Row 30: K2, (Sl1, K1, PSSO) K across = 17 (18, 20, 21, 22) sts.

Row 31: BO 2 sts, P across the row =15 (16, 18, 19, 20) sts.

Row 32: K2, (Sl1, K1, PSSO) K across = 14 (15, 17, 18, 19) sts.

Row 33: P across the row.

Continue in St st until piece measures 15.5 (16, 16.5, 17, 18)"/39 (40.5, 42, 43, 46)cm.

BO loosely.

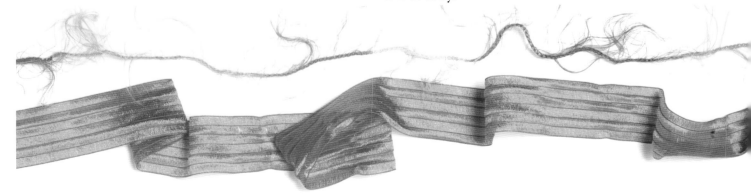

Left Front

With 1 strand of *Jungle*, CO 21 (22, 24, 25, 26) sts.

Rows 1–3: Work in Garter stitch pattern.

Row 4: K across.

Row 5: Join 1 strand of *Viola* yarn and P across the row.

Rows 6–27: Beginning with a K row, work in St st stitch for 22 rows.

Row 28: K across to last 3 sts, K2tog, K2 = 20 (21, 23, 24, 25) sts.

Row 29: P across the row to last 2 sts, BO 2 sts =18 (19, 21, 22, 23) sts.

Row 30: K across to last 3 sts, K2tog, K2 = 17 (18, 20, 21, 22) sts.

Row 31: P across the row to last 2 sts, BO 2 sts 15 (16, 18, 19, 20) sts.

Row 32: K across to last 3 sts, K2tog, K2 = 14 (15, 17, 18, 19) sts.

Row 33: P across the row.

Continue in St st until piece measures 15.5 (16, 16.5, 17, 18)"/39 (40.5, 42, 43, 46)cm.

BO loosely.

Sleeves (two pieces)

With 1 strand of *Jungle*, CO 36 (38, 40, 42, 46) sts.

Rows 1–4: K across.

Row 5: Join 1 strand of *Viola* yarn and P across the row.

Row 6: K1, *YO, K2tog* repeat from * to * across, end K1.

Row 7: P1, *YO, P2tog* repeat from * to * across, end P1.

Repeat rows 6 and 7 five times.

Row 18: K across.

BO loosely.

Finishing

Join shoulders with back, position sides seams together, and sew using the Mattress stitch with *Jungle* yarn. Sew sleeve seams together.

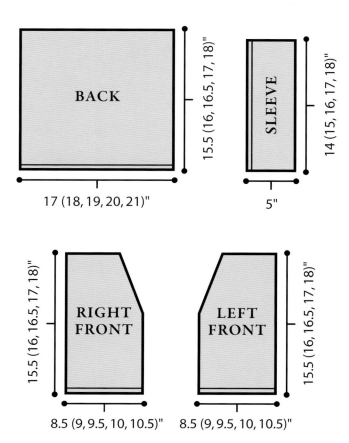

BACK

15.5 (16, 16.5, 17, 18)"

17 (18, 19, 20, 21)"

SLEEVE

14 (15, 16, 17, 18)"

5"

15.5 (16, 16.5, 17, 18)"

RIGHT FRONT

LEFT FRONT

15.5 (16, 16.5, 17, 18)"

8.5 (9, 9.5, 10, 10.5)"

8.5 (9, 9.5, 10, 10.5)"

Beaded Handbag

ADVANCED BEGINNER

We can never have enough handbags, and this one tops the list of must-have accessories. This versatile purse is knit with denim suede-like yarn to create a durable yet soft fabric. Midnight blue glass beads add a rich textural surface. The easy shoulder strap features a decorative, selvage edge. Great for a special party or everyday wear.

Yarn

4 balls Berroco *Suede* 120yds (111m)
50g (100% nylon) Color: #3704

Needles & Materials

US #6 (4.00mm) needles or size needed to obtain gauge.
520–Size E glass beads

Finished Measurements

9" (23cm) wide x 6.5" (16.5cm) long.

GAUGE

In Stockinette stitch pattern, 21 sts and 35 rows = 4" (10cm).

STOCKINETTE STITCH PATTERN

Row 1: K across.

Row 2: P across.

Repeat rows 1 and 2.

SUBSTITUTION YARNS

Berroco *Suede* = GGH *Velour*

NOTES

❋ For added support, trim double thick fusing for the size of the Gusset, place in bottom, and sides of bag.

❋ To close the bag, attach a snap on the inside of the Front Flap.

❋ For a color variation, work the Back Flap in a different color yarn.

Beaded Handbag Pattern

Front

String 360 beads onto the *Suede* yarn and CO 49 sts.

Row 1: K across.

Row 2: P across.

Begin A Bead Pattern:
Row 3a: *K1, place bead, K1*, repeat from * to * to end.

Row 4a: P across.

Row 5a: K2, *place bead, K1, repeat from * to last 2 sts, K2.

Row 6a: P across.

Continue in A Bead Pattern and repeat Rows 3a–6a for 2.25" (6cm) (end on Row 6).

K across row.

P across row.

Begin B Bead Pattern:
Row 1b: K1, place bead, K2, place bead, *K3, place bead, repeat from * to last 4 sts, K2, place bead, K1.

Row 2b: P across.

Row 3b: K across.

Row 4b: P across.

Row 5b: K2, place bead, *K3, place bead, repeat from * to last 2 sts, K2.

Row 6b: P across.

Row 7b: K across.

Row 8b: P across.

Continue in B Bead Pattern and repeat Rows 1b–8b for 4.25" (end on Row 8b).

BO loosely.

Back

String 156 beads onto the *Suede* yarn and CO 49 sts.

Work in St st for 1.25" (3cm) without beads.

Back Flap

Begin A Bead Pattern:

K across row.

P across row.

Row 1a: K2tog, *K1, place bead, K1*, repeat from * to * to last 3 sts, K1, K2tog.

Row 2a: P across.

Row 3a: K2tog, K2, *place bead, K1, repeat from * to last 2 sts, K2, K2tog.

Row 4a: P across.

Continue 4 rows A Bead pattern. Dec 1 st each end, every row, until 1 st remains.

BO loosely.

Gusset

Bottom Gusset

Working 2 strands of *Suede* held tog, CO 17 sts.

Work in the Garter stitch pattern for 9" (23cm) to match bottom width of bag.

Side Gusset

Dec 1 st, K2tog each end every 10 rows, 5 times until 7 stitches remain for strap.

Strap

Slip the 1st stitch as if to Purl, K across. Repeat for every row until 36" (91cm) or desired length.

Side Gusset

Inc 1 st each end every 10 rows, 5 times until 17 stitches remain for strap.

BO loosely.

Finishing and Assembly

Align gusset bottom with front bottom and sew together. Align gusset left side with front right side and sew together. Repeat for gusset right side and front left side. Repeat for back. Sew cast on edge of gusset to bind off edge to secure corner of purse.

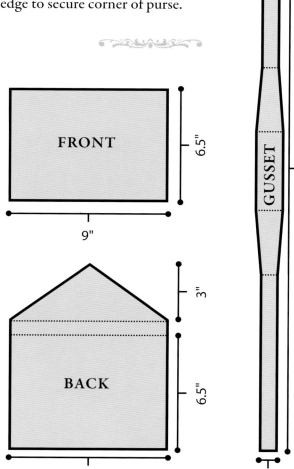

Cozy Capelet

ADVANCED BEGINNER

This classic capelet is the perfect off-the-shoulder wrap that you'll want to show off all weekend long. Velvety soft, superfine cashmere wool is paired with sassy mohair, and features a delicate ruffle edging. Change needle size for super-easy shaping without decreasing. A perfect match with the Easy Skirt (page 78).

Yarn

2 (3, 3, 4) balls S. Charles *Ritratto* 198yds (180m)
50g (53% viscose, 28% mohair, 10% polyamid, 9% polyester) Color: #77

2 (3, 3, 4) balls Karabella Yarns *Boise* 163yds (150m)
50g (50% cashmere, 50% superfine merino wool) Color: #61

Needles & Materials

One pair each of US #10 (6mm) and US #8 (5mm) needles
or size needed to obtain gauge.

Sizes

S (M, L, XL) Instructions are for smallest size,
with changes for other sizes in parentheses.

Finished Measurements

Chest: 36 (38, 40, 42)"/91 (96.5, 101.5, 106.5)cm.
Length: 16.5" (42cm).

GAUGE

In Stockinette stitch pattern, 18 sts and 24 rows = 4" (10cm) with 1 strand each of *Boise* and *Ritratto* held tog, with US #10 needles.

STOCKINETTE STITCH PATTERN

Row 1: K across.

Row 2: P across.

Repeat rows 1 and 2.

2 x 2 Ribbing Stitch Pattern

Row 1: *K2, P2. Repeat from * to end of row.

Repeat this row

SUBSTITUTION YARNS

S. Charles *Ritratto* = Ironstone Yarns *Paris Nights*

Karabella Yarns *Boise* = Debbie Bliss *Cotton Cashmere*

NOTES

❋ Hand wash only. Lay flat to dry.

❋ Join yarns at the end of a row.

❋ Add a color coordinated fabric pin for an added embellishment.

Cozy Capelet Pattern

Front or Back (two pieces)

With 1 strand each of *Ritratto* and *Boise* held tog, CO 160 (172, 180, 188) sts.

Ruffle

Rows 1 and 2: K across.

Beginning with a Purl row, Drop *Ritratto*, and continue in St st for 2" (5cm) ending with a Purl row.

Next Row: K2tog across the row = 80 (86, 90, 94) sts.

Join 1 strand of *Ritratto*, and continue in St st for 7.5" (19cm) from beg.

Drop *Ritratto*, change to US #8 needles, and continue working in St st with 1 strand of *Boise* for 4" (10cm) from beg.

Inc 0 (2, 2, 2) sts across the row = 80 (88, 92, 96) sts.

Top Band

Work in Ribbing stitch pattern, for 3" (7.5cm).

Finishing and Making the Neckline

Position the front and back side-by-side on a flat surface, wrong side up. Sew side seams with *Boise* yarn. Fold the bind off (top edge) in half. Let the elastic band hang over the sides. Do not trim. Using *Boise* yarn sew the top band over the elastic. Be careful not to sew into the elastic. Sew other side seam except top band opening. Stretch elastic 1" (2.5cm) from top band and sew together with strong thread. Trim ends. Sew side seam of top band.

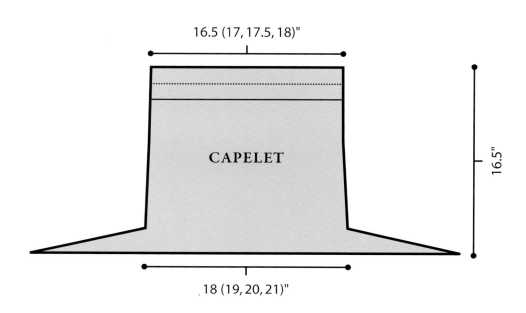

16.5 (17, 17.5, 18)"

CAPELET

16.5"

18 (19, 20, 21)"

Easy Skirt

ADVANCED BEGINNER

Get a head start on the new season with this huggably-soft, ruffle-trimmed skirt. Knit in a Stockinette stitch pattern, this hip skirt is a wonderful blend of soft cashmere and mohair yarns. It features an elastic waistband for a kicked-back casual fit. Add the Cozy Capelet (page 74) for a sizzling, matching set.

Yarn

2 (3, 3, 4) S. Charles *Ritratto* 198yds (180m)
50g (53% viscose, 28% mohair, 10% polyamid, 9% polyester) Color: #77

2 (3, 3, 4) Karabella Yarns *Boise* 163yds (150m)
50g (50% cashmere, 50% superfine merino wool) Color: #61

Needles & Materials

US #10 (6mm) needles or size needed to obtain gauge.

Sizes

S (M, L, XL) Instructions are for smallest size,
with changes for other sizes in parentheses.

Finished Measurements

Hips: 36 (38, 40, 42)"/91 (96.5, 101.5, 106.5)cm.
Length: 17.5" (44.5cm).

GAUGE

In Stockinette stitch pattern, 18 sts and 24 rows = 4" (10cm) with 1 strand each of *Boise* and *Ritratto* held tog.

STOCKINETTE STITCH PATTERN

Row 1: K across.

Row 2: P across.

Repeat rows 1 and 2.

2 x 2 RIBBING STITCH PATTERN

Row 1: *K2, P2. Repeat from * to end of row.

Repeat this row

SUBSTITUTION YARNS

S. Charles *Ritratto* = Ironstone Yarns *Paris Nights*

Karabella Yarns *Boise* = Debbie Bliss *Cotton Cashmere*

NOTES

✳ Keep track of the stitches for the cast on with stitch markers, every 10 stitches. Remove markers when working the 1st row.

✳ Join yarns at the end of a row.

✳ Hand wash only. Lay flat to dry.

Easy Skirt Pattern

Front or Back (two pieces)

With 1 strand each of *Ritratto* and *Boise* held tog, CO 174 (184, 194, 202) sts.

Ruffle

Rows 1 and 2: K across.

Beginning with a Purl row, Drop *Ritratto*, and continue in St st for 2" (5cm) ending with a Purl row.

Next Row: K2tog across the row = 87 (92, 97, 101) sts.

Next Row: Inc 14 (14, 14, 15) sts across the row = 101 (106, 111, 116) sts.

Join 1 strand of *Ritratto*, and continue in St st for 10" (25cm) from beg.

Next Row: Dec 17 (19, 19, 20) sts across the row = 84 (87, 92, 96) sts.

Continue in St st for 14.5" (37cm) from beg.

Next Row: Dec 3 (3, 4, 5) sts across the row = 81 (84, 88, 91) sts.

Waistband

Work in Ribbing stitch pattern, for 3" (7.5cm).

BO loosely.

Finishing and Making the Waistband

Lay the knit skirt on a flat surface, wrong side up. Sew one side seam with *Boise* yarn.

Place flat elastic band along the waistband and fold the bind off (top edge) in half. Let the elastic band hang over the sides of the skirt. Do not trim. Using *Boise* yarn sew the waistband over the elastic. Be careful not to sew into the elastic. Sew other side seam except waistband opening. Stretch elastic 1" (2.5cm) from waistband and sew together with strong thread. Trim ends. Sew side seam of waistband.

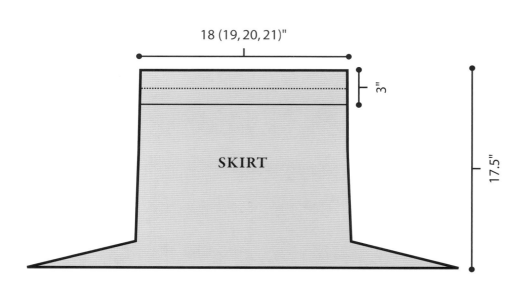

18 (19, 20, 21)"

3"

SKIRT

17.5"

Lace and Beaded Top

ADVANCED BEGINNER

Create a beautiful mix of beads, and accent with a scalloped-lace edge, for a perfect finishing touch. You'll want to be seen around town in this sassy, must-have, comfy pullover, knit in a trouble-free Stockinette stitch pattern. The stylish design, and sheer quality of this high visibility top will make it one of your favorites.

Yarn

5 (8) balls Debbie Bliss *Cathay* 108 yds (100m)
50g (50% cotton, 35% viscose microfiber, 15% silk) Color: #12011

Needles & Materials

US #6 (4mm) needles or size needed to obtain gauge.
117–Size E clear iridescent glass beads

Sizes

S-M (L-XL) Instructions are for smallest size,
with changes for other sizes in parentheses.

Finished Measurements

Chest: 36.5 (42.5)"/93 (108cm).
Length: 16.5 (17.5)"/42 (44cm).

GAUGE

In Stockinette stitch pattern, 24 sts and 32 rows = 4" (10cm).

STOCKINETTE STITCH PATTERN

Row 1: K across.

Row 2: P across.

Repeat rows 1 and 2.

SUBSTITUTION YARNS

Debbie Bliss *Cathay* = Patons *Grace*

NOTES

* If the *Cathay* yarn is too thick to pass through the eye of the needle, lead the yarn through with a finer thread.

* Join yarns at the end of a row.

* Hand wash only. Lay flat to dry.

Lace and Beaded Top Pattern

Back (one piece)

With 1 strand of *Cathay*, CO 110 (128) sts.

Rows 1–3: K across the row.

Row 4: P across the row.

Scallop Border

Row 5: K1, *K2tog 3 times, [YO, K1] 6 times, K2tog 3 times, repeat from * across row to last 2 sts, end K1.

Row 6: P across the row.

Row 7: K across the row.

Row 8: P across the row.

Row 9: K1, *K2tog 3 times, [YO, K1] 6 times, K2tog 3 times, repeat from * across row to last 2 sts, end K1.

Row 10: P across the row.

Row 11: K across the row.

Row 12: P across the row.

Row 13: K1, *K2tog 3 times, [YO, K1] 6 times, K2tog 3 times, repeat from * across row to last 2 sts, end K1.

Work in St st for a total of 9.5" (24cm) from beg, end on a P row.

Armholes

Next row: BO 2 (3) sts at beg of the row, K across the row = 108 (125) sts.

Next row: BO 2 (3) sts at beg of the row, P across the row = 106 (122) sts.

After BO, Continue in St st for 3" (8cm), dec 1 st evenly across last row = 105 (121) sts.

Next row: Work in Garter stitch pattern for 4 rows.

Shoulder Straps

Next row: K6 (place sts on a stitch holder) BO 93 (109) sts, K6.

Join a second strand of *Cathay* yarn.

Knit shoulder straps individually, bring yarn forward as if to Purl, Slip 1st stitch onto right needle, and bring yarn back to knit position. Knit across.

Work even for 4 (5)"/10 (13cm).

BO loosely.

Front (one piece)

With 1 strand of *Cathay*, CO 110 (128) sts.

Rows 1–3: K across the row.

Row 4: P across the row.

Scallop Border

Row 5: K1, *K2tog 3 times, [YO, K1] 6 times, K2tog 3 times, repeat from * across row to last 2 sts, end K1.

Row 6: P across the row.

Row 7: K across the row.

Row 8: P across the row.

Row 9: K1, *K2tog 3 times, [YO, K1] 6 times, K2tog 3 times, repeat from * across row to last 2 sts, end K1.

Row 10: P across the row.

Row 11: K across the row.

Row 12: P across the row.

Row 13: K1, *K2tog 3 times, [YO, K1] 6 times, K2tog 3 times, repeat from * across row to last 2 sts, end K1.

Work in St st for a total of 9.5" (24 cm) from beg end on a P row.

Armholes

Next row: BO 2 (3) sts at beg of the row, K across the row = 108 (125) sts.

Next row: BO 2 (3) sts at beg of the row, P across the row, dec 1 st evenly across row = 105 (121) sts.

Cut yarn, string 117 beads, and join yarn.

Bead Pattern (*see page18, Knitting with Beads)

Bead row: K across to 51st (59th) st, *place bead, K1, place bead, K1, place bead,

K across the row = 3 beads

Next row: P across the row.

Bead row: K across to 50th (58th) st, place bead, K1, place bead, K1, place bead, K1, place bead,

K across the row = 4 beads

Next row: P across the row.

Bead row: K across to 49th (57th) st, place bead, K1, place bead, K1, place bead, K1, place bead, K1, place bead, K across the row = 5 beads

Next row: P across the row.

Bead row: Knit across to 48th (56th) st and continue in bead pattern = 6 beads

Next row: P across the row.

Bead row: Knit across to 47th (55th) st and continue in

bead pattern = 7 beads

Next row: P across the row.

Bead row: Knit across to 46th (54th) st and continue in bead pattern = 8 beads

Next row: P across the row.

Bead row: Knit across to 45th (53rd) st and continue in bead pattern = 9 beads

Next row: P across the row.

Bead row: Knit across to 44th (52nd) st and continue in bead pattern = 10 beads

Next row: P across the row.

Bead row: Knit across to 43rd (51st) st and continue in bead pattern = 11 beads

Next row: P across the row.

Bead row: Knit across to 42nd (50th) st and continue in bead pattern = 12 beads

Next row: P across the row.

Bead row: Knit across to 41st (49th) st and continue in bead pattern = 13 beads

Next row: P across the row.

Bead row: Knit across to 40th (48th) st and continue in bead pattern = 14 beads

Next row: P across the row.

Bead row: Knit across to 39th (47th) st and continue in bead pattern = 15 beads

Next row: P across the row.

Next 4 rows: Work in Garter stitch pattern.

Shoulder Straps

Next row: K6 (place sts on a stitch holder) BO 93 (109) sts, K6.

Join a second strand of *Cathay* yarn.

Knit shoulder straps individually, bring yarn forward as if to Purl, Slip 1st stitch onto right needle, and bring yarn back to knit position. Knit across.

Work even for 4 (5)"/10 (13cm).

BO loosely.

Finishing

Sew shoulders together. Position and sew side seams.

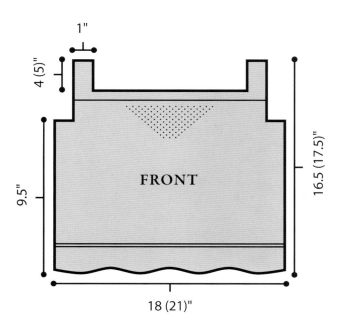

FRONT

1"

4 (5)"

9.5"

16.5 (17.5)"

18 (21)"

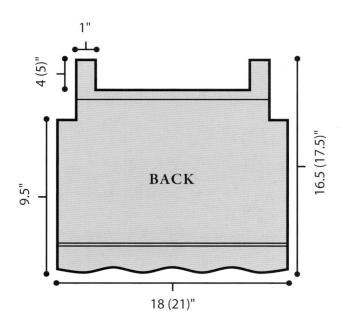

BACK

1"

4 (5)"

9.5"

16.5 (17.5)"

18 (21)"

Sassy Shrug

ADVANCED BEGINNER

Like a basic black dress, everyone needs a little black shrug to complete their fashion wardrobe. Dress it up or go casual with jeans. The sassy shrug has easy ruffle ties and flair sleeves. Knit from a cotton and soft mohair blend, this mini sweater is great to wear for all seasons.

Yarn

4 (4, 5, 5, 6) balls Rowan *Calmer* 175yds (160m)
50g (75% cotton, 25% acrylic) Color: #465

5 (5, 5, 6, 6) balls GGH *Soft-Kid* 150yds (138m)
25g (70% super kid mohair, 25% nylon, 5% wool) Color: #027

Needles & Materials

US #11 (8mm) needles or size needed to obtain gauge.

Crochet hook

Sizes

XS (S, M, L, XL) Instructions are for smallest size,
with changes for other sizes in parentheses.

Finished Measurements

Chest: 34 (36, 38, 40, 42)"/86 (91, 96.5, 101.5, 106.5)cm.
Total Length: 15.5 (16, 16.5, 17, 18)"/39 (40.5, 42, 43, 46)cm.

GAUGE

In Stockinette stitch pattern, 13 sts and 17 rows = 4" (10cm) with 2 strands of *Calmer* and *Soft-Kid* held tog.

GARTER STITCH PATTERN

Knit every row.

STOCKINETTE STITCH PATTERN

Row 1: K across.

Row 2: P across.

Repeat rows 1 and 2.

SUBSTITUTION YARNS

Rowan *Calmer* = GGH *Java*

GGH *Soft-Kid* = Filatura Di Crosa *Multicolor*

NOTES

✳ If you choose to knit the shrug with only 1 yarn, pick a yarn that matches the stated gauge.

✳ Block to size before assembly.

✳ Hand wash only. Lay flat to dry.

Sassy Shrug Pattern

Right Front

With 1 strand each of *Calmer* and *Soft-Kid* held tog CO 94 (96, 97, 99, 101) sts.

Ruffle Tie

Rows 1–3: Work in Garter stitch pattern.

Row 4: K2tog for 20 sts, K across row = 84 (86, 87, 89, 91) sts.

Row 5: K across.

Row 6: K2tog for 50 sts, K across = 59 (61, 62, 64, 66) sts.

Row 7: K across.

Row 8: BO 32 sts, K across = 27 (29, 30, 32, 34) sts.

Body

Rows 9–13: (WS) Work in St st pattern.

Row 14: K2, (Sl1, K1, PSSO) K across = 26 (28, 29, 31, 33) sts.

Work Rows 15–33: St st across. Every 4th row K2, (Sl1, K1, PSSO) K across = Rows 18, 22, 26, 30

Row 34: K2, (Sl1, K1, PSSO) K across = 21 (23, 24, 26, 28) sts.

Shaping Armhole

Row 35: P across.

Row 36: K across.

Row 37: P across.

Row 38: K2, (Sl1, K1, PSSO) K across = 20 (22, 23, 25, 27) sts.

Work Rows 39–54: St st across. Every 4th row K2, (Sl1, K1, PSSO) K across = Rows 42, 46, 50, 54.

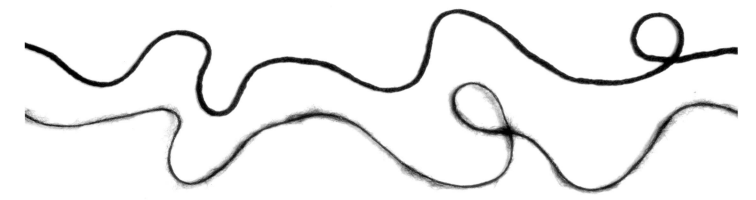

Row 55: P across.

Row 56: K across = 16 (18, 19, 21, 23) sts.

Row 57: P across.

Row 58: K2, (Sl1, K1, PSSO) K across = 15 (17, 18, 20, 22) sts.

Row 59: P across.

Row 60: K2, (Sl1, K1, PSSO) K across = 14 (16, 17, 19, 21) sts.

Row 61: P across.

Row 62: K2, (Sl1, K1, PSSO) K across = 13 (15, 16, 18, 20) sts.

Row 63: P across.

Row 64: K across.

Row 65: P across.

(RS) Continue working in St st until piece measures 15.5 (16, 16.5, 17, 18)"/39 (40.5, 42, 43, 46)cm.

End on Purl row.

BO loosely.

Left Front

With 1 strand each of *Calmer* and *Soft-Kid* held tog CO 94 (96, 97, 99, 101) sts.

Ruffle Tie

Rows 1–3: Work in Garter stitch pattern.

Row 4: K across, K2tog 20 sts = 84 (86, 87, 89, 91) sts.

Row 5: K across.

Row 6: K across, K2tog 50 sts = 59 (61, 62, 64, 66) sts.

Row 7: K across.

Row 8: K across, BO 32 sts = 27 (29, 30, 32, 34) sts.

Body

Rows 9–13: (WS) Work in St st pattern.

Row 14: K across to last 3 sts, (K2tog, K2) = 26 (28, 29, 31, 33) sts.

Work Rows 15–33: St st across. Every 4th row: K across to last 3 sts, (K2tog, K2) = Rows 18, 22, 26, 30

Row 34: K2, (K2tog) K across = 21 (23, 24, 26, 28) sts.

Shaping Armhole

Row 35: P across.

Row 36: K across.

Row 37: P across.

Row 38: K across to last 3 sts, (K2tog, K2) = 20 (22, 23, 25, 27) sts.

Work Rows 39–54: St st across. Every 4th row K across to last 3 sts, (K2tog, K2) = Rows 42, 46, 50, 54.

Row 55: P across.

Row 56: K across = 16 (18, 19, 21, 23) sts.

Row 57: P across.

Row 58: K across to last 3 sts, K2tog, K2 = 15 (17,18, 20, 22) sts.

Row 59: P across.

Row 60: K across to last 3 sts, K2tog, K2 = 14 (16, 17, 19, 21) sts.

Row 61: P across.

Row 62: K across to last 3 sts, K2tog, K2 = 13 (15, 16, 18, 20) sts.

Row 63: P across.

Row 64: K across.

Row 65: P across.

(RS) Continue working in St st until piece measures 15.5 (16, 16.5, 17, 18)"/39 (40.5, 42, 43, 46)cm.

End on Purl row.

BO loosely.

Back

With 1 strand each of *Calmer* and *Soft-Kid* held tog CO 55 (58, 61, 64, 67) sts.

Rows 1–8: work in Garter stitch pattern.

Continue in St st until piece measures 15.5 (16, 16.5, 17, 18)"/39 (40.5, 42, 43, 46)cm.

End on Purl row.

BO loosely.

Sleeves (two pieces)

With 1 strand of *Calmer* and *Soft-Kid* held tog CO 52 (54, 54, 54, 56) sts.

Rows 1–3: K across the row.

Row 4: K1 (0, 0, 0, 2), *K1, K2tog repeat from* across row = 35 (36, 36, 36, 37) sts.

Row 5: K across the row.

Row 6: K2 (3, 3, 3, 2), K2tog twice, *K1, K2tog*, repeat from * to * to last 2 sts, K2tog = 23 (24, 24, 24, 25) sts.

Row 7: K across the row.

Row 8: K across the row.

Row 9: (WS) P across the row.

Continue in St st, Inc 1st each and every 4th row 16 times until sleeve measures 17.25" (44cm) or desired length. Sleeve is fashioned to extend into center of hand.

BO loosely.

Finishing

Join shoulders with back, position sides seams together, and sew using the Mattress stitch with *Calmer* yarn. Sew sleeve seams. With crochet hook, beginning at bottom of right front, work a single crochet in approximately every other stitch up the right front, and right neck opening. Single crochet in every stitch along back neck edge, tighten at corners. Proceed down left front to match right side.

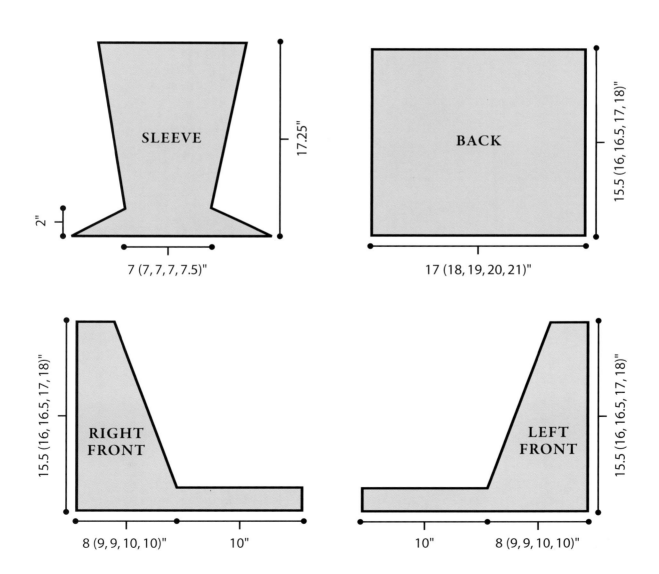

SLEEVE

17.25"

2"

7 (7, 7, 7, 7.5)"

BACK

15.5 (16, 16.5, 17, 18)"

17 (18, 19, 20, 21)"

RIGHT FRONT

15.5 (16, 16.5, 17, 18)"

8 (9, 9, 10, 10)"   10"

LEFT FRONT

15.5 (16, 16.5, 17, 18)"

10"   8 (9, 9, 10, 10)"

Skill Level Project Guide

EASY - Garter and Stockinette stitch patterns without shaping.
BEGINNER - Garter or Stockinette stitch patterns with easy shaping, and minimal assembly.
ADVANCED BEGINNER - Garter, Stockinette, and decorative stitch patterns with defined shaping and assembly.

Fringed Wrap 30

Jazzy Belt 34

Beaded Flip-flops 38

Mini-Jelly Bag 54

Vintage Camisole 42

Boa Jelly Purse 50

Jelly Beach Bag 54

Chenille Bag 58

Chenille
Ruffle Top 62

Ruffle Poncho 46

Spring Sweater 66

Beaded Handbag 70

Cozy Capelet 74

Easy Skirt 78

Lace and
Beaded Top 82

Sassy Shrug 88